Love,
Kasey

THE MONEY MAP

A Spiritual Guide for Financial Success

By
Kasey J. Claytor

Disclaimer

There are no specific recommendations for any particular investment in this book, but merely ideas and methods of encouraging a good financial education, including investing. This book does not approve, instruct, or support any specific recommendations of any investments or legal direction to individuals. The reader should consider all factors when making informed decisions. Individual situations vary and this book offers general guidelines that may not be appropriate for everyone. Kasey J. Claytor is not legally responsible for investment decisions or legal documents made with respect to any information presented in this book or other distribution mediums.

The author of this book does not dispense medical advice or prescribe the use of any technique as a form of treatment for physical, emotional, or medical problems without the advice of a physician, either directly or indirectly. The intent of the author is only to offer information of a general nature to help you in your quest for emotional and spiritual well-being. In the event you use any of the information in this book for yourself, which is your constitutional right, the author and the publisher assume no responsibility for your actions.

Osprey Publishing
Type Design and Typography: Morin Design
Cover Design: Morin Design
Photo of Author: Robeson Photography
ISBN 978-0-692-89050-9
Printed in the United States of America

To my son, Justin Wade
Who is forever with me,
Of whom I'm forever proud,
Who established himself
In abundance and love.

Praise for The Money Map

"In this book, *The Money Map*, Kasey Claytor blends great spiritual knowledge and values with her expertise on everything financial. If you've ever wondered why you can't seem to breakthrough to more prosperity, I think this book is for you. Solid financial guidance mixed with mind/body/spirit principles to raise your 'money consciousness' as Claytor has defined it. It's whole-health for your financial wellbeing."

> – **Mark Anthony**, JD, Psychic Explorer (aka The Psychic Lawyer® Psychic Attorney and Psychic Adventurer), is a world-renowned psychic medium. He is the author of the critically acclaimed spiritual bestsellers *The Afterlife Frequency, Evidence of Eternity* and *Never Letting Go*.

"*The Money Map* is way more than a book...it is an experience of having a wise and compassionate mentor standing next to you and taking you by the hand. As your personal ally you'll find Kasey Claytor to be a strong and steadfast champion while, at the same time, she is absolutely real and vulnerably transparent as she shares about her own dark night of the soul money moments.

The cumulative effect of participating in *The Money Map* journey is one of feeling simultaneously challenged and inspired. Use every bit of practical reaching beyond your current imaginings of what might be possible for you."

> – **Elyse Hope Killoran**, Prosperity Coach and creator of the multidimensional *"Anchoring Prosperity"* CD.

"With warmth, humanity and insight, Kasey Claytor invites readers on a transformative journey towards heightened money consciousness. *The Money Map* offers a relatable guide that delves into the interconnected realms of the non-physical and the material.

Whether you're seeking to elevate your money mindset or harmonize your financial journey with your personal growth path, this book is a wonderful companion. Kasey's personal story resonates long after the final page, leaving you equipped to embrace a more conscious, inspired and empowered relationship with money."

– **Hema Vyas**, The Omnipreneurial Psychologist™

"Have you ever wondered how you got to where you are financially, and why? Would you like to find the financial freedom you so long for? Would you like to know how to be a successful investor? Or do you just want to be able to manage your finances a little better? If you said "yes" to any of these, Kasey Claytor offers this comprehensive guide to reaching the financial stability that is possible for us all.

She begins by introducing 10 Levels of Money Consciousness. Clearly and compassionately, she explains what is experienced at each level, and how to start moving up the financial ladder.

If you're investing or want to, she offers extensive guidelines and pointers to help you avoid unnecessary pitfalls. She does this so you'll know what you are doing and why.

Charts, exercises and affirmations are included to support you in every stage of this process.

According to Kasey (and the many luminaries with whom she has studied), our financial situation is always affected by our habitual thinking and beliefs. In other words, what goes on inside goes on outside.

That is why Kasey sees financial success both as a practical and a spiritual goal. We don't often hear that, or even understand how spirituality could fit into our picture until we realize that our financial health isn't just about money.

You see, money isn't the total answer. What we really want is to be happy. That is why Kasey asks you to look at your thoughts and feelings, beliefs and fears, because this journey is really about discovering yourself. When you find "that," the answers—and the peace you long for—will be there, too.

Brilliantly yet thoughtfully written, this book has something for everyone, regardless of their financial status. Highly recommended!"

> – **Donna Miesbach**, Certified Chopra Global Meditation & Yoga Instructor, Award-winning Poet & Author

Table of Contents

Introduction

I was raised in a comfortably middle-class family for the first twelve years of my life. We had a nice eleven room, two story, colonial tucked in a neat tree-lined street, with broad sidewalks and wide, green lawns. We looked much like the families from the 1950s that were on TV at the time, like *Father Knows Best* and *Leave it to Beaver*.

Then something happened. My father, who had a real estate firm with 80 agents, a big office and healthy income, *lost it all*. I will never know all the details of what happened. He passed away soon after I left home, so I never got the opportunity to talk with him about it, adult to adult. I do know he worked too much, and he lived large, so it is enough for me to know that he was out of balance. Even so, he and I had many special, magical times where he shared his beliefs about life. He was always optimistic, believing he would get back on top again, become a millionaire, but even though he worked hard he never managed to reclaim his former successes.

My teenage years were a mix of humiliation, increasing poverty, and loneliness. Dad, Mom, and my sister and I moved to the other side of town, where the homes were older and smaller. It was a time where things didn't make sense to me, and I didn't have the life skills to understand what was happening. When I was in ninth grade we moved to Florida into a small apartment and there was often no money to pay for my school lunches. I was embarrassed and tried to hide it from others. It felt like I didn't even know who I was anymore.

I married young for the obvious reasons; I was anxious to grow up and take some control of my life.

My husband was a good man who was dependable, and we eked out a sufficient lifestyle on his pay. I stayed home with our two sons; happy our young family had a little bit of financial independence, and I took pride in learning how to make do with what we had. I was able to squeeze in my college classes then too. When times were hard financially, I went into what I called my pioneer mode; making everything that we needed from scratch. I made clothes, homemade cereal, built shelving, and children's beds; I would try anything. *But I always had this vision*; I had this *vivid vision* of prosperous times. I saw myself sitting behind a desk, neatly dressed, while I helped and counseled people in some way. It was always there, even as I stood in the food stamp line to help my mother apply for aid after my father passed away, even when my husband got laid off and we both took any odd, labor-intensive jobs, even when, after I got divorced, and my mother died, after I lost my job, and found a care package of canned goods on my front porch; *even then*. This vision saw me through. As I grew into my thirties, I had a lot of catching up to do. I scrambled to learn all the little pieces of etiquette I'd missed because after Dad died my mom was a mess. I had attended our local college, but I had to quit when my mother got ill, and I was the only one available to care for her. I didn't even *own* clothes appropriate for office work.

I drew from what little I remembered of the Sunday afternoon conversations with my father. And he had said *I could do or be anything I wanted*. I wanted to get into the world of business. And from what I remembered my father telling me, I was only held back by what was going on in my head.

So, what did I want? *I had a dream of finishing my father's dream.*

In my twenties, while living in my own world raising young boys, I relished taking the time to read books about child development, natural foods, psychology, the Seth books, Science of Mind and all the great ancient religions! Since my teens, I've been studying and gathering knowledge on how spirit and mind works. It took time; I was a slow reader, especially back then. Yet reading slowly, going over the paragraphs until they became crystal clear to me, meant I was really digesting and integrating the material. It stayed with me.

I did succeed. Every step toward my vision brought a new celebration; every failure brought disappointment, yet I can see how it was a necessary part of the plan. All that time I was actively incubating my vision. I'm not saying it was simple, but what I have learned through all the successes and failures is that it always starts in our thinking and beliefs. God, the universe, has incredible treasures for us, surrounding us, right now. I learned we have been given the raw material to create the world we see in our dreams. We can hone our instincts to steer us in the right direction. We can stir up the passion inside of ourselves that we never knew we had, and those passions are there as an impetus to our personal fulfillment which includes abundance.

At the age of 31, with both of my children in school, I was eager to start my career. About this time I went through a divorce, and found I needed to work a few menial jobs first, but my eyes were always on getting into the world of business!

Events unfolded beautifully. I found a job selling advertising (that was fun), and I was told to find a sponsor for the stock market report on a radio station. Naturally I went into a brokerage office to offer them the chance to sponsor it. The manager was very nice but not convinced. He sent me to his boss. In the end it turned out they were considering me for the position of stockbroker. They liked my selling style; no pressure, congenial. I was floored when I realized what this meant for my future!

So, there I was in a completely new world. I began playing the game I thought the brokerage industry expects in corporate society. I needed to understand how everything worked together in the 'real' world. Even with my previous mind/body/spiritual interests, my soul-seeking-self became submerged because of my focus on fitting in, and not understanding fully how the spiritual principles I had learned could not only be useful, but necessary in my success. A part of me was taking notes all along, knowing I would go back to my spiritual beliefs and combine all this information with deeper meaning. For the next twenty odd years I kept my beliefs to myself at work, fearing mainstream businesspeople would judge me as weird or 'new age'.

I never liked the term 'new age'. It seems to be a grab bag description of anything that suspiciously veers away from mainstream views, anything new, different, and not understood. I studied Christianity, Judaism, Buddhism, Hindu, etc. I find them all so very beautiful. I love them because at their core they represent love and all of our highest potential qualities.

What do I teach now all these years later? I teach that if you fully integrate the spiritual lessons into your financial life, as I explain through this book, you may heal your financial health. We exist in the physical world as bodies, but we also exist emotionally, intellectually, and energetically. Our financial lives are connected to the rest of ourselves. If we are to have total wellbeing it must include the financial part. After all, how can we be happy, clear thinking, productive, and full of vitality, if we are stressed about bills we can't pay, and needs we cannot meet?

The Purusharthas, mentioned in the Indian Vedic texts, are a large body of religious writings by ancient, enlightened seers. They list four aims of life: that of purpose, (Dharma), material security, (Artha), pleasure and relationships, (Kama), and freedom, self-realization, (Moksha). Even the great sages of India knew without material security we will have deficits in our wellbeing. Artha is the security of having the material resources we need to live in the world with ease. It is a basic human dignity. And for any of us to take care of our families without money crises, it's necessary to have material balance.

Financial success is a spiritual goal.

But what about the money?

Who doesn't want more money? When asked, all of us would say, "Of course," but what does money mean in our lives? What if we had a map to guide us toward financial health?

How did money get such a bad reputation? Why do so many people beat themselves up over how much or how little they have? Why do we tend to see wealthy individuals as somehow corrupt?

Money flows in and out of our lives like some big, quiet secret. We want more, yet we keep it out of reach by holding negative views of it and refusing to learn about it. We have those little nudges that we should learn more about its properties, but just thinking about it puts knots in our stomachs. We are attracted to its benefits—all those shiny things—and of course the security it represents. But at the same time, we see and hear about how some people misuse it; use it for the wrong reasons, and cause harm by their greed and dishonesty. In the media and the movies, rich people are often portrayed as selfish or worse, evil.

Money can terrify us if we are honest with ourselves. Thinking of its loss in our lives may leave us feeling vulnerable, and fearful, as if the ground will give way beneath us. I'll bet most people find it is just too much to think about. A current, popular idea is to hold positive thoughts. Yet negative thoughts about money keep coming back, because the source of our anxiety isn't ever fully addressed.

A basic feeling of safety and confidence is essential for us to have fulfilling lives. We can't experience wellbeing without it. *Total wellbeing includes the absence of money worries.* Remember Artha, an important aim of life. Everyone will occasionally be concerned about their own finances, but overall, if you have wellbeing, you don't awaken in the middle of the night panicking about money.

This book is about helping you reach that place where you aren't overly concerned about your financial future; to find that place within yourself that guides your decisions toward your highest good. By gaining more self-awareness such as learning more about where your beliefs and attitudes come from, you will have the information to make better choices. You can imagine future outcomes with reasonable accuracy, you have the courage to take risks, knowing the trepidation will pass, and the risks will bring rewards. You can comfortably move among different circles of people no matter what their income level. You wake up with your own song in your heart, inspired to prosper in your own unique way.

You can arrive at that place by raising what I call your Money Consciousness. Like any evolutionary step, money consciousness can be pinpointed on a graph. The Map of Money Consciousness™ begins at

Level 1, represented by apathy and little awareness of responsibility for your own circumstances, all the way to Level 10, where you are completely supported emotionally and financially by your passions. You can easily find yourself on this map and it really helps to clarify your next step.

This book will guide you through the levels of money consciousness. I've arranged it in such a way that you will gently be led toward greater awareness of money and wellbeing. Each chapter is divided into three sections under that chapter's theme; each theme will be discussed from a spiritual, physical, and financial point of view. By breaking it down this way we take the mystery out of money, showing it as just an extension of the mind/body/spirit dynamics. We begin with the broad view of the universe and its infinitely creative attributes, look at our life in the physical world and its magnificent duality, and end with the penny in our pocket. With this approach, we see our own individual multidimensional reality and how much dominion we have over it.

Every tiny baby step in the direction of higher consciousness, or awareness, takes us into new worlds of perception. Consciousness at its most basic definition is being aware of one's own existence. "I think. Therefore I am." quoted by Rene Descartes in 1637. It is much more than that, however. Does a bird have consciousness? A dog? Sentient beings, we agree, have some form of awareness they do exist. In humans we can observe different levels of awareness, which we will refer to in the following pages. Every incremental shift in consciousness holds new magical qualities in our lives. Every such shift, with a new focus and a basic knowledge of how money behaves, gives us a fresh new feeling of wellbeing—a wellbeing that includes peace of mind. Consciousness can be quantified, measured on a scale showing higher and higher levels of understanding, leading to different perceptions of reality, and increasingly intuitive knowledge which ultimately creates more peace, understanding and success. The level of consciousness you are operating on right now colors everything you perceive in the world and in your thinking. In fact, readers with differing levels of consciousness can read a book and come away with entirely different takes on it!

You will learn that where you are right now is perfect. You don't need to lambaste yourself for what has happened in the past, because we are all doing our best at any given moment from the awareness that we have at the time. Wherever you find yourself in your financial life, feeling guilt about it isn't productive. Letting go of guilt can bring fresh ideas, new energy, and intentions. We will work on forgiveness because it is a powerful release. Could we be holding prosperity back due to feelings of unworthiness which forgiveness would settle? We are all innocent. Every day is a new start-over.

Please, as you move through this book; as you read, take the quiz, or fill out the worksheets, do so with a sense of compassion for yourself. Take the quiz and do the exercises when you feel moved to. Make it easy on yourself. This is not a college course that ends in 6 weeks. You can take 6 months if you like! Take small steps, and take them one at a time. If you break the journey down into small segments, you will be less overwhelmed, and you are more likely to grow. (And ascend the Map of Money Consciousness™!)

I want you to prosper financially, but not at the expense of your wellbeing. We see this every day; people putting a high value on acquiring wealth while at the same time losing their sense of peace. I've seen it up close with clients both ways. I've taught leaning into this light of wellbeing and watched it in others naturally unfold. Total wellbeing includes physical, emotional, spiritual, and financial, *balance*.

There is something magical about money—the way it appears and disappears, grows and shrinks, and, in a similar way of taming a hesitant wild horse, with calm assuredness and confidence, not only will you learn to control it, but you will find you can joyfully master it.

Let's go forward and find success and indeed happiness in all areas. You deserve every good thing in this life. Keep heart and mind open, and breathe—all is well.

A Brief Introduction to the Map of Money Consciousness™ and the Money Map Quiz

The Map of Money Consciousness™

Most people want to be successful and have more money but aren't sure how to get there. I realized one day I could develop a map for them. Anyone can find what level they are presently on; thus, easily know what the next step is.

The Map is a scale designed to explain the different levels of your understanding about how money works. Each individual will have a different experience of understanding money at different consciousness levels. What determines a position on the scale is a combination of habitual thinking, beliefs, raw intelligence, and emotional intelligence. When these traits are combined, you can see a developing financial maturity. For true fulfillment in the highest way that includes life harmony (beliefs, desires, and purpose all blending to support each other) one needs to have a well-defined understanding of human behavior, intra- and inter-relationship competence, financial knowledge, confidence in self, and inspired action.

I have been intrigued by the theories of different scholars, great thinkers, and philosophers of our time on the subject of consciousness and the evolution of society. We can easily transfer these concepts to the different areas of our lives. Remember the four aims: purpose, security, enjoyment, and freedom.

I've read and applied those theories to raise my own awareness about human nature and life in general. My career since 1983 has been to create wealth for people. It rang so true to me upon reading and pondering the works of people like Dr. David Hawkins *(Levels of Human Consciousness)*, who devised a way to measure levels of consciousness from 1 to 10. In Dr. Hawkins scale, at level one we find someone whose basic drive for survival is a main motivation, around three and four are the beginnings of honesty and commitment to promises, all the way up to ten which is the level of a purely enlightened human. Then there is Dr. Don Beck and Clare Graves *(Spiral Dynamics)* who devised a way to measure levels of functioning for individuals, organizations, and societies, explaining ways to evolve in leadership, problem solving and decision making. Also, Ken Wilbur *(Integral Psychology)*, who is the founder of the Integral Institute, formed in collaboration with over 200 scholars and experts. They specialize in education, politics, business, medicine, psychology, spirituality, as well as law and criminal justice. He elaborates further on *Spiral Dynamics*.

It dawned on me one day, in a quantum leap of understanding, that money consciousness could be measured on a scale, just like any other evolutionary behavior or mode of thought. This scale would be helpful to people who want to increase their financial success because they could see where they are now and what their next step would be.

No matter where we find ourselves on the Map of Money Consciousness™, or what our life situation is, we can raise ourselves up to where we want to be, where we dream of being. Every step on the map is important; the knowledge gained from each transcended level builds a foundation upon which to launch to the next level. So, where we are right now, in this very moment, is exactly right for us. This is where we are supposed to be—everything that has happened in the past, where we came from and everything that we have ever thought—has landed us right here. It is from here we can begin.

We so often look way, way out on the horizon and declare, "I want to be over there!" Eagerly, we motivate ourselves to action. It seems, after so much action, that the goal is still too far off, too unattainable. Our doubts begin to creep in, undermining our original enthusiasm, leaving us daunted and overwhelmed with the enormous gulf between where we are now and where we'd like to be. How do we get there? We hear how other people do it but there are as many opinions on the hows as there are people telling us. And, if we really examine our goals, we don't want just money, we want to be happy. We want to feel fulfilled, purposeful, secure, and free from despair.

This Map is designed from the knowledge and experience I've acquired from working with people from all different backgrounds; watching their successes and failures, coaching them into a new understanding of what a wealth consciousness is, and helping them see the roadblocks that they themselves place in their paths. Showing them that where they are now is OK, they can already see how far they have come, and they begin again with a new commitment that will carry them to financial peace of mind. Financial success is a consequence of a well lived life. It is so interwoven with all other aspects of life, that some ideas may seem removed from finance, yet it is integral, and should be incorporated.

What follows is the Money Map quiz that will show you where you are on the scale right now. It is also on my site, kaseyclaytor.com. You can take it now and once again when these concepts begin to make sense to you.

Map of Money Consciousness™ Quiz

This is a short quiz designed to give you a snapshot of your level right now on the Map of Money Consciousness™. Write down the numerical value to each response and add the total of each level. Try not to think too much about the answers but go with your first impulse. To agree with a statement, it should be your current thought pattern.

0 = no, never or strongly disagree   **4 = fairly often, mostly agree**
1 = seldom or disagree   **5 = frequently, agree**
2 = sometimes   **6 = yes, always, strongly agree**
3 = equally yes and no

LEVEL 1

1. You find yourself blaming others for your circumstances. _____

2. You find yourself thinking there should be more help from the government, your employer, or someone else. _____

                                        Level 1 Total: _____

LEVEL 2

3. Thinking about money makes you anxious. _____

4. You find yourself in a financial crisis. _____

                                        Level 2 Total: _____

LEVEL 3

5. You like to dream of an abundant life, but think it's unlikely to come true. _____

6. You find yourself envying those who have wealth. _____

                                        Level 3 Total: _____

LEVEL 4

7. You feel frustration or anger because you aren't as far financially as you would like to be or feel you should be. _____

8. You've recently been feeling ready to take on the challenge of getting your finances in order. This is a new improvement from previously feeling overwhelmed or apathetic. _____

Level 4 Total: _____

LEVEL 5

9. You have a new feeling of inspiration to be more proactive in your financial health. _____

10. You are becoming interested in learning about ways to invest, have a retirement plan, and want to do more now. (If you've held that interest for a long time, it would be a low score.) _____

Level 5 Total: _____

LEVEL 6

11. You find yourself paying attention to financial or economic information (economic news, magazines, financial planning) and have a sense of financial discipline, i.e. good credit, good budgeting, and impulse control. _____

12. You are optimistic about your future; you're mostly satisfied with your financial status, and money worries are beginning to fade, but you know you must remain vigilant. _____

Level 6 Total: _____

LEVEL 7

13. You *now* know you did the best you knew how to in the past. You forgive yourself for the mistakes you've made, and you don't blame anyone else. _____

14. You understand your credit score, cyclical nature of the economy, and how the market functions. _____

Level 7 Total: _____

LEVEL 8

15. You're good at anticipating possible results of taking risks in business or investments and are more comfortable with risk-taking in general. _____

16. You have a strong sense of purpose in life and a passion for your chosen endeavors. There is harmony between your values, desires, and actions. These actions provide your income. _____

Level 8 Total: _____

LEVEL 9

17. You feel financially abundant along with a great emotional satisfaction with your life. _____

18. You are comfortable with your financial decisions and don't worry about making an income. Your business or investments provide whatever you need or want. _____

Level 9 Total: _____

LEVEL 10

19. You feel there isn't any more you need, you've found your life's purpose and it is generously supported. _____

20. You feel money isn't a focus because so much abundance surrounds you and always will. It seems as if the whole world conspires to support you. _____

Level 10 Total: _____

12	
11	
10	
9	
8	
7	
6	
5	
4	
3	
2	
1	

LEVELS   1   2   3   4   5   6   7   8   9   10

On the graph above draw a vertical bar to the correct height for each of your totals. Most likely there will be one bar that sticks up prominently and that represents where your money consciousness is operating, for the most part, in your life. If you have two prominent bars that are next to each other, you are probably in transition from one level to the next.

Short bars to the left of the prominent bar represent earlier levels (values), that you have transcended. You don't function there much anymore, yet you draw from the knowledge you attained in those levels. The degree that you succeed in these levels depends on how well you mastered each and how you've been able to retain and utilize that knowledge. Short bars to the right of your prominent one/ones represent the money consciousness that you have not yet embraced. There is not a right or wrong stage, a good or bad stage; all levels have value as you progress on your path.

Here is a brief description of the levels of money consciousness. What determines a position on the scale is a combination of habitual thinking, beliefs, raw intelligence, and emotional intelligence. When these are combined you can see a developing financial maturity. For true fulfillment that includes financial 'harmony' (beliefs, desires, and purpose all blend) one needs to have a well-defined understanding of human behavior, intra and inter-relationship competence, economic knowledge, confidence in self, and inspired action. At the end of the book there are Keys to rising to the next level. Retake it when you have completed the book.

Level One

Blame/Despair/Apathy

You find yourself in poverty, unemployed or meagerly employed, and have the world view of a victim on the stage of life. You feel helpless to change circumstances. You blame your situation on others; family, employer, community, 'you', or government. You are resigned to this reality and don't have any hope it will change. It is extraordinarily difficult to raise oneself out of this level, though with a life changing event you may transcend it. Here, if one happened to win the Lottery it would most likely be gone within two years. You have no money skills and lack the necessary emotional skills as well. You feel the world is conspiring against you. Wealthy people are viewed in mythic proportions; it isn't 'real life' to you.

Level Two

Fear/Anxiety

You are more aware of your situation and have an idea that you 'should' be able to do better, yet you have fear of the unknown, fear of taking chances and anxiety over change. This is a big hurdle for people in this category. These fears can all be unconscious; you feel anxiousness surrounding money but can't quite define what is holding you back. This mindset corresponds with a lack of trust in life's ability to sustain you. You are limited by habitual thinking and see a way out only in magical terms. You don't have faith in yourself having the ability to create a comfortable life. Perhaps you learned this from parents or other significant adults as you were growing up. You resist feeling hopeful so you don't become disappointed. When money happens to come to you it seems to slip right through your fingers. You are financially in chaos.

Level Three

Desire/Craving

At this level people are moving beyond apathy and debilitating fear, so desires naturally spring up. Instead of deadening your desires or withdrawing away from them, you welcome them into your awareness. You like to entertain ideas and begin to dream of a grander way of life. Money naturally becomes more of a focus in your plans. Checking and savings accounts are becoming mastered, as well as steady employment. You find yourself in a situation of denial for the bulk of your desires, however, because you still lack the basic knowledge about money that will enable you to accomplish more. Your resentment of others who have more success is still present and interestingly, that holds you back, because people don't envy someone else unless they believed themselves unworthy.

Level Four

Anger/Aggression

At this level there is a dramatic change because you are becoming more aware of the part you play in your own life. At this level anger shows up that gives you the energy to change your situation. The apathy is gone. It takes an enormous amount of effort to rise out of a Level Three lifestyle to a higher one. The anger you feel is usually projected out onto others but is most likely from anger at yourself. You now realize that you, and only you, must take action. One must be aggressive to overcome all the obstacles and learn the rules of money. The anger gives the impetus at this level that will make it possible to continue up the scale.

Level Five

Courage/Optimism

There is relief here. There is great hope and a feeling of inspiration. Budgeting is mastered. Better employment, a retirement plan, and a healthy curiosity about how money works have become part of the fabric of your life. You've crossed a defining line where financial disasters are less frequent. Your *curiosity* about money is protection against the common financial mistakes people make. Not only have you learned about banking and retirement planning, but you're now looking at other ways to make your money grow. Your ears are open and you're thinking about ways to manifest more financial security. Though you still have trepidations, you feel empowered. **Financial Health** is emerging.

Level Six
Satisfaction/Trust

At this level people are understandably satisfied. You are learning how to build financial security, maximize your earnings through saving and investing, and building good credit. You are careful with purchases and investments. You have mastered delaying gratification which is a necessary component on the way to financial independence. You are beginning to experience the freedom a sustainable faith in your future brings. You know your future is in your own hands and feel up to the challenge. You trust yourself and trust your growing knowledge, but you are still a bit hard on yourself, thinking you should do more, know more, and so on.

Level Seven
Acceptance/Forgiveness/Giving

Now we are beginning to move on the downside of the bell curve. The people that have risen to this level are discovering how the economy really works. You've begun to develop a more complete understanding of the free market system, mortgages, credit card companies, and taxes, and are secure in your chosen career. You can look back at your own past choices and understand that you did the best you could with the information you had at that time. Now you can accept your current situation, assess where you want to go, and implement a long-term financial plan. You know your talents, strengths, and have a sense of purpose. You have a forgiving attitude toward yourself and others. You are able to recognize what makes people financially successful and can plainly see why some fail. Blaming others for your situation is not likely by this stage. And a new generosity is emerging that goes beyond giving to the family by extending outward to community and charity. Peace surrounding your finances is possible for this and the upper levels.

Level Eight

Wisdom/Abstraction/Reason

Wisdom is knowledge that is internalized and becomes a part of you. It becomes innate. When this is developed on the subject of economics, one can successfully run scenarios of financial undertakings through his or her head, playing the "What will happen if..." game. Creative expression coupled with finance and business becomes common here. Failures certainly can occur because one gave it a shot, but here again—a person at this level knows there will be no gain without risk. Until this stage, ventures into business ownership are often unsuccessful. The wisdom with which to sense various outcomes isn't completely matured until level eight. There is an expansive understanding of human nature which is essential in successful commerce. Here is also a stronger desire to serve, and a passion for your chosen field is present.

Level Nine

Self-Actualization

One now understands the deeper meanings surrounding money, and how emotions play such an integral role in one's experience with it. A person at this level has mastered the emotional side of money. One assumes a feeling of security and no longer worries about material things. You can invest with confidence, review, and adjust financial plans, create an estate plan, and participate in some type of service. You've often learned the skill of creating a flow of income that is not dependent on your actions; the money comes in whether you show up at work or not. This is called passive income. Business owners, real estate investors, and security investors, can fit in here if you have achieved true meaning and purpose in your lives.

Level Ten

Illumination

Money becomes a natural means to support one's *purpose*. As this person goes out into the world money isn't a focus at all. People flock to support this type of person because of what they represent: hope, knowledge, and inspiration. Great religious leaders, great teachers and other types of conscientious leaders are carried on a wave of contributions. Some who attain this level are overcome with greed and fall back several levels. Some on this level retreat happily to live with or without large amounts of money. They have truly 'transcended' their material desires.

Of course, most of you who are reading this will fall somewhere in the middle. Just getting to 6 or 7 is a ***real accomplishment***. Having a map can show you where you might want to go. If you want to go to the next level, hang out with others that are on that one, find a good coach and regularly assess your goals.

Chapter 1

Clearing

Getting Rid of What Isn't Working
Once and for All

*"You know you've achieved perfection in design, not
when you have nothing more to add, but when you
have nothing more to take away."*
– Antoine de Saint Exupéry

Clearing away space in your life for time to learn about money and the
security it brings is necessary for your financial success. There are also
many other things we can clear away that will open the path for you,
making it easier to improve financially. Attitudes could be obstacles,
like getting overwhelmed and continually putting things off. But when
we invoke our spiritual side into the mix, giving us a higher level of
knowledge and confidence, and eliminate all that is getting in our way,
well now, we may just be unstoppable.

Don't think you have to put in a huge effort to live prosperously;
it's our natural state and we can subtract things from our life that will
uncover our abundance. Abundance is a description of Nature, *All That Is*.
We find our lives can quickly fill up with everything but abundance—
with scarcity, unfulfilled desires, envy, and suffering. With mindful,
patient and steady care, we can learn to ignore the negative traffic in

our mind. We are not our thoughts and we can learn to stop paying so much attention to them!

As you begin the process of clearing away what you don't want, you will notice the pieces of your life falling into more order, setting goals with intention and attention affecting your reality. Most importantly, discovering who you really are inside, what will fulfill you, and give you peace and joy.

Nothing is kept from you, nor hidden from you. It is all plainly in sight—all your answers to the where, how, and why of prosperity and happiness, and what that means to you.

Learning about money consciousness by looking at it through three different lenses, physically, spiritually, and financially gives you insight into your current financial life. This in turn helps you gain even more knowledge with which to change where you are and move toward where you want to be. The map can guide you there!

So where do you start?

We can eliminate the wasteful actions and wasteful spending that we are aware of. As we mature, we eventually figure out what is really necessary for our fulfillment and what we need for our wellbeing; what gives us contentment and peace of mind that's not dependent on outside conditions. You will discover where there is waste in how you spend *time* as well as money, and how you spend your gifts, your creativity and passions. When you want to buy something, ask yourself if it is moving you in the direction of who you really are. Or if you are just motivated to move toward who you think you are supposed to be? Look around and see what to eliminate by assessing whether these things or activities separate you further from your inner-self. We all have an innate sense of 'knowingness' working within us, and you can learn to connect to this and find the answers.

While you're eliminating unproductive ideas and actions, you can also reduce bad habits that have crystallized themselves into material forms like credit card debt! It is fairly common for people to use credit cards to their detriment, such as delaying a more serious financial problem that isn't honestly faced. These, like clutter, impede the flow of life energy. It's like tapping on the brakes of your financial life.

Once you become aware of the worries of the ego (*all* worries are of the ego), your decisions concerning your financial choices, investments, objectives, and sources of advice will be clearer.

Our three Sections under the Topic of Clearing:

Spiritually, *eliminate those ideas and judgements that are not of abundance.*

Physically, *eliminate waste, obstructions, and unproductivity.*

Financially, *comb through your asset placement, cleaning up the financial clutter.*

> ***Spiritually***, *eliminate those ideas and judgements that are not of abundance.*

For your spiritual, non-physical self, how do you eliminate ideas and beliefs that are not productive for creating prosperity? Thoughts of doubt come from your ego. If you look beyond the ego, you find your Higher Self, the spiritual part of you connected to the unmanifest or field of consciousness. As you learn to foster this connection it can help you in all areas of your life, including the financial.

Throughout the last century, quantum physicists conducted a vast array of experiments where they studied and tested what underlies all of reality, they call the *Field*. The Field is an invisible force that has no form, yet pervades all space, time, and matter like an energy net binding all events, things, and even our thoughts into one colossal organized, intelligent Field. This Field holds life's unlimited potential. It transcends any distance or time instantaneously. Scientists conducting experiments have shown the far-reaching effects of this Field in many instances. One prominent example is seen in how plants show a reaction when other plants are under duress. The stress of plants when other plants were being cut has been well documented even when the plants were *several hundred miles apart.*

A neuropsychologist, Karl Lashley, was one such scientist. He had studied the brain for twenty years and decided to find out exactly where memory resides. He had read of the results of other scientists like Wilder Penfield, who had shown that if certain parts of the brain were stimulated with electrodes, scenes would be evoked in the patient's mind in great detail. But it never answered the question of where exactly the memories are held in the brain. This led them to consider that our thoughts and memories may lie beyond the physical world, held in what is called non-local reality.

Our individual thoughts, memories, and reactions to outside events are processed through our ego, which is our sense of self, the "I". Our ego enables us to learn how the material world operates and consequently we learn how to survive. As we grow, we identify so intimately with our ego that we aren't aware of our larger selves, (which you may call your soul, spirit, or higher self). The ego is just the operating system for our perceptions in this dimension, and it is our job to bring it back to that. Unnecessary fear and suffering is caused when we identify too exclusively with our ego, and believe that our thoughts are the totality of what's possible. Our own ego mistakenly leads us to believe that we are vulnerable, at the mercy of whatever the world throws at us, leaving us struggling in chaos. Operating solely from the ego, we feel blind-sided by things that appear to have little sense in our daily lives like the weather and the stock market trends. But underneath this limited awareness is a smooth still energy of All That Is. By being more aware, we can rope in the ego and align with our spirit, limiting the worries and anxieties that occupy our egos.

When I was a teenager, I worked in a movie theatre and loved sitting up in the projection room with the giant projector. I'd watch the grey celluloid film clicking through the lens, passing the small but intense point of light. From that little light sprang a world of big color, sound, and motion twenty feet high. We can now hold a small flash drive that is basically inert, but once it is put into a device, the point at which the drive connects springs forth a story with color, sound, people, and motion. On the drive *where there is no contact, nothing is happening.* It is for our past and future—it's inert or plastic on the flash drive!

The divine undercurrents of our life hum along below the ego. The universe, God, is pointing a light through us, and at any given moment we are expressing our own creation. It is important to understand the function and limits of the ego. If we recognize what is merely a perception of the ego, we can differentiate those from our *Higher Self, or who we really are.*

When your thoughts are me-centered: angry, frightened, or anxious, they lead to emotional turmoil. You naturally view the world and outside events normally through your ego. This can lead to suffering when you experience what you don't want. Having only this perspective is painful because you're not consciously aware of your source, God, and that underlying peace—but your ego tells you that "I," your identity in its entirety, is made up solely of your physical form, your personality, and the thoughts in your mind. You're probably saying, "That is all well and good, but I don't see what my ego has to do with money!"

We aren't talking about "money," a hollow symbol of trade; we are talking about *your money.* When I was a new, young broker, it wasn't too long in the business before I discovered how attached people are to their money. It struck me then that asking them to allow their money to be handled by another person was equivalent to asking them to hand over a very personal part of themselves. And in a sense, it is. We've become quite attached to our physical being, which at its very essence is nothing but energy (scientists have broken it down to particles that blink on and off, emitting energy), so yes, your money is another extension of your *expression* here. We are so very attached to our financial situation because it is tied to our self-worth or lack of self-esteem, depending on how much we have or think we should have.

Right now, you are experiencing the culmination of your past thoughts. Remember the old saying, "If you always think what you have always thought—you'll always get what you've always got."

In our culture today our attention is almost completely outward; we are heavily influenced by what we see and hear. We are on default, reacting to events instead of consciously participating in the creation of our lives. We've forgotten how glorious, mysterious, and magical we are! Without being aware of it, we buy into the ads that tell us what will make us beautiful, popular, thin, happy, wealthy and successful. We want that. Without thinking, we buy into all of the hype and consequently become dissatisfied if we don't have the beautiful car, the thin, toned body, the youthful, smiling family—and we reach out, searching for that thing which will bring satisfaction. Buying those products briefly satisfies us until we find a new goal to seek. This just leads us on a never-ending cycle of desire, attainment, and ultimate dissatisfaction again. Even lottery winners move back to their 'everyday' state of mind—their set point of the previous level of contentment three months after their winnings. They end up as happy or unhappy as they were before!

The first step to ending this process is to become aware of your attention, thoughts, and beliefs. Connecting to that still self, your true identity, and observing from that perspective, will give you a huge jump toward improving your life in every way. Listen to the thoughts running wild through your mind second-by-second, minute-by-minute, and you'll see a continual chatter of judgments, worries, self-blame and maybe angry thoughts. Newcomers to meditation are usually astonished to realize how pervasive these thoughts are when they sit and attempt to calm their minds. Every time you catch yourself and observe these wild ramblings, you are hopping over to that part of you that is the *observer*. The observer is your inner being that is connected to All That Is. It is here that you are free from troubles, regrets, and anxiety. This is where you can create that joyful, prosperous life that unfolds effortlessly. Sakyon Miphom, a Buddhist monk, likens our thoughts to wild horses. In his book, *Turning the Mind into an Ally*, he creatively explains how we tame the mind in the same fashion that we would tame a wild horse, keeping our thoughts in line with the path of happiness like training a horse to stay on the trail.

Much of our thinking is habitual, stemming from our beliefs and assumptions. I call this 'rut' thinking. Years ago, I had a client, an older woman who, after losing her husband, had to re-learn to drive. For years after she and her husband retired, he always drove. Therefore, in her mind, driving had become a dangerous feat, the worst of which was turning left onto a two-way road, crossing the oncoming traffic—so she refused to do that. For the rest of her life, she only went where she could turn right, making a small or a large circle back home. She only went to stores and businesses that fell on this pattern. When I called her to ask if she could come down to the office, she explained that was impossible because she would have to make a left turn. Not only was her accessible world limited, but her thinking was in the same rut as her driving. Believing left turns were impossible limited her experience.

In this same way, we each limit our experience with thinking that is based on the belief that we can't. But that, again, is only our ego speaking because we are really not restricted. Our divine origin is waiting for us to fully express our abundant, joyful nature, and we easily do just that when we learn to transcend the ego. The paradox is that we operate through the ego to rid ourselves of the ego's grip on our reality!

Our thoughts are simply manifestations of our beliefs and attitudes. We are all familiar with this idea, yet one of our core beliefs could be that change is very difficult! The good news is you can learn new tools to replace old thinking with thoughts that are in harmony with health, happiness, and abundance.

So again, the first step is to become aware of those thoughts that limit your prosperity. You are already glorious, incredible, vibrant, miraculous, clever and genius. All those things that are not true about you are just your ego which so convincingly tells you what you must do to become nicer, stronger, better looking, more successful, richer, smarter, etc. All these qualities are yours already. Your ego is forever dissatisfied.

As you move through your day, catch yourself when you are telling yourself you can't have something or do something. Notice if envy pops up when meeting prosperous people. Envy is simply stating you can't be like them. Trace that jealousy to the belief it came from. You may feel shame when you come across a poor person. Does that come from a belief that it's wrong if you have more? As Dr. Wayne Dyer, renowned author and speaker in the field of self-development, said, improving your life and reaching for your abundance does not take that away from others.

Our egos are continuously thinking, (50,000 thoughts per day!) and our decisions are usually based on them. Most of them are repetitious, the same thoughts as yesterday. Left unchecked we live haphazardly from moment to moment. We may think of some concern and end up telling ourselves stories about it, thus making it into a 'big' problem, when in fact there really was none to begin with. We have created an imaginary future situation, like worrying we won't perform well at a task at work, or that we'll make a bad impression, or the investment we funded will tank. Some counselors call this disaster planning. How many times a day do we do this? Our point of power is right *now*. It is the only thing that is real. All change we want to effect must occur in our now, our solutions are found in the now. If we dwell on our past mistakes, lacks, and failures we are creating more of the same in our future. As said in many ways by ancient sages and modern spiritual leaders, *'What you pay attention to grows'*.

If we are to attain financial health as well as success in other areas of our lives, we must know who we are, how we are keeping ourselves from what we want, what we really desire and why, and finally, how to get what we desire.

Most of us are going in circles, like the rut thinking of the widow. Or like the stock market when it stays in a trading channel; that is, it goes up and down in a defined range, never breaking through the ceiling nor falling through the floor. We may rise to experience a bit of prosperity only to fall back to old habits of thinking and actions that sink us back down to our 'normal' or default existence. Just as we do research to find a good location to live in, or a good investment to buy, we can research the landscape of our minds—and how rich, mysterious, and rewarding that is! In knowing ourselves well, we acquire the information we need to eliminate those thoughts that are not aligned with prosperity. We will then be able to use intention and attention to fulfill our dreams.

> ***Physically***, *eliminate waste, obstructions,*
> *and unproductivity.*

To the extent that you can freely, joyously give of yourself, abundance will flow effortlessly and very naturally into your life. All of nature is this way. The cycle of water upon the earth, the ground growing food and giving up its yield nourishing animal life; why, birds don't run out of insects and we don't run out of sunshine! There is a continual flow that never ceases. Even the stock market depends on a steady stream of those buying and those selling, ebb and flow. Abundance circulates.

When we grab and cling to stuff or money, we stop the flow because we think it won't come to us again. This behavior is fighting nature. Holding on creates stagnation. A physical expression of this is clutter, a crammed closet, or a stuffed drawer. Notice how you feel opening a jumbled, messy closet. In the ancient oriental art of *Feng Shui*, clutter is an obstacle to the natural flow of energy that is all around us. Upon clearing a home of all the energy-draining clutter, people universally notice a new lightness of being, an openness that clears the mind as well as the personal space.

You may want to spend a weekend or two going through your possessions and deciding what you don't need, what may be draining your energy, and what brings you joy. We can surround ourselves at home and at work with the things that we absolutely love. Things that remind us of a loved one, things that have beauty and colors that enliven us, things that speak of our passions and create an ease; these are so good for us. Let's eliminate—give away or throw away—items like that ugly ceramic pot that you've been keeping only because it was a gift and you thought you should. Get rid of things that remind you of past unpleasantness. When looking at them you can feel your mood drop a bit—and the farther you drop in mood, the more resistance you have to that flow of energy. We want that energy to have a clear path. This drop in mood is actually a drop in your vibration. A higher vibration is more aligned with your inner being, who you really are, and is accompanied by that blissful feeling. Rid your home of all the items you never use! Have a garage sale! It is amazing what we hang on to in our physical reality just like those negative beliefs. Embrace those thoughts that speak of positive, prosperous living and multiply the cherished joyful things in our lives. Surround yourself with an abundance of beauty.

There is a great book by Karen Kingston called *"Clear Your Clutter with Feng Shui"*. I highly recommend it for this exercise. Even if you only follow the first few chapters, I think you will notice higher vibrational energy coming your way. Of course, we feel better with more order, more openness; it gives us more clarity. Working in clutter feels as if our minds are functioning underwater. Working in an orderly environment with lots of open space, surrounded by objects we enjoy, allows the water to evaporate and the lightness can clean the fog from our minds!

We also can look at the *time* we have and how we decide to use it. We don't often realize the wealth of time we have available to us. If we look closely, we all have a lot of 'fillers' in our day. Some are important to us— the things we do to unwind, activities that don't require much of us like shows, movies, games, or google. Upon examination, these activities are drawing our attention out and away from ourselves. In some instances, while we engage with our devices, we are drawn out and into others' experiences, and while this can be cathartic, it doesn't really enable us to find out who we really are or create any change in our circumstances. Perhaps we can reduce this type of activity and replace it with activities conducive to a positive life change. Let go of some of these reflex activities and new doors will open as our attention awakens to new ideas.

Inspiration (in-spirit) comes from that invisible, divine dimension. The constant flow of energy available to us from the origin of life, from the divine field, carries our passions and unlimited creativity. We are receivers of nudges, insights, and clues to where our successes lie. We can only become aware of these when we clear the path and calm the ego so we are able to notice. We open an avenue for these messages when we carve out time to be quiet as in meditation and prayer, and when we move in the direction of activities we are passionate about (those that seem to give us more energy and a sense of timelessness).

How you spend your time also reveals how you feel about yourself. In your gut you know how much you care about yourself, just as your family and friends can tell if you are really enjoying the time you spend with them. You're giving yourself messages continuously, and if you are not enjoying your own company by always seeking outward entertainment, outward stimulation, and social situations, you could be using your time to the exclusion of finding your own inner desires. Think back to incidences that happened when you were young, or a teenager or even young adult, that resulted in a negative voice in your head saying you weren't smart, or lovable, or important.

If you only take the time to meet who that person is in the mirror, you will see that you are magical. You were created in great detail from your unique DNA to become an exquisite, elaborate form from God's own essence. You are designed to create. Your life can be a journey filled with abundance that allows you to express your gifts and talents. This is where you will find your wealth. Love yourself where you are now with all your complications.

There is a way to acquire wealth while enjoying the path and taking the time to show yourself some tender caring and acceptance. Trust that divine wisdom gave you all you need to fulfill every desire. The universe began 13.7 billion years ago, and every spark of energy and information within it is in an infinite process of expressing that manifested glory—*of which you are a part*. You are endowed with the impulse to create. With every thought and action, you rule your universe!

If it is at all possible, spend some quiet time by yourself. Maybe early in the morning you could journal. Limit your TV time. Build in some time to enjoy nature and daydream. These are the activities that foster insight, ideas, and creativity. By clearing your physical space and opening up more 'spiritual' time, what you are really doing is moving away from time-wasting activities that have frozen your progress. Once you begin tapping into your insightful *SELF* you are forever changed. And you will have more time to move in a new direction with the new ideas you're receiving. This is a consciousness-raising path!

> ***Financially***, *comb through your asset*
> *placement, cleaning up the financial clutter.*

Before we delve into the financial world, I want to recognize that this leap from the spiritual domain to the world of hard currency may seem vast and cumbersome to travel. In my earnest attempt to make this transition I've had to move from the paradigm of the spirit to the paradigm of the ego. But the same rules flow in the undercurrents of both worlds. There is really no separation, so bear with me as I enter the world of money, as illusory as it is!

How close do you pay attention to the money you have now? Do you gather all your change and use it? Or take it in rolls to the bank? Or is it spread throughout your home like metal cobwebs in drawer corners, dressers, and pockets? It's easy to disregard small coins and bills, yet added together they are significant.

A friend came into my office one day and told me he had an elderly neighbor he was helping out, and he discovered something very surprising in her home. She was becoming frail so he offered to help her clean up her place. When he was putting something in the closet, he found a stock certificate sticking up out of a brown grocery bag. On closer examination he realized the whole bag was crammed with more stock certificates! He came in to ask me if I could help her straighten it all out. He continued to find more certificates as the days went by and repeatedly brought them down, with her, to my office until we were sure we had them all, including uncashed dividend checks. All totaled, she had several hundred thousand dollars' worth of stocks carelessly thrown in paper bags, while living like a pauper!

Of course, this is an extreme scenario; I just want you to see how far someone can overlook their own prosperity. It's easy to fall into thinking that it won't be enough to matter, but money is money. Are we telling the universe we don't really care about it? It's all the same energy and when we keep adding it together, we build momentum, and each time we acquire a new quantity we shift gears and it becomes easier, just like shifting while riding a bike. And the momentum, fueled by our attention, increases.

Let's use Feng Shui with our money. Not only gather all our forgotten change but take inventory of all our assets and liabilities. Write them all down on a sheet of paper or type them up. If you have life insurance or annuities with any cash value, don't forget to put these down too. They also are assets.

We are not going to worry about what your net worth is now, (assets – liabilities 'debt' = net worth), that isn't important at this moment. Rather, we are going to focus on organizing the financial energy you generated in your past. This is our base. We are going to take the care you put into acquiring what you already have, and couple that with the enthusiasm you are introducing into your life now. Harnessing those two positive strategies allows you to generate new energetic thought patterns into the universe, which in turn results in the building blocks of your success.

Take a good look at your overall financial picture. Does your gut tell you that this is probably where you will continue to stay? Do you feel anxiety or even fear when you look at it? Do you feel pride, or a sense of gratitude? This is part of your relationship with yourself and what you think you are worth. This accounting is an outward manifestation that is mirroring your inner financial health. And you can change it if you want to. Developing an inner awareness of the how and why in the beliefs that led you to your present situation will help you move in the right direction. So, use this information as a tool to understand why you are here, and then we will work on where you can envision going.

In practical, worldly terms let's see what you have manifested. Let's embark on the task of financial housekeeping. Do you have small balances at various institutions? Do you have small mutual fund and stock accounts that you tend to ignore because they are so small? Examine not only these orphaned accounts but also small life insurance policies that you may not need anymore. I have had new clients come into my office with statements from 25 to 30 different bank accounts, stock accounts, retirement accounts, annuities, mutual funds and life insurance policies! It would be a full-time job just to keep up with all of them! There are reasons to have several accounts if you are wealthy and you have several million dollars in cash. Banks typically will insure through FDIC (Federal Insurance Deposit Corporation) protection only up to $250,000 per customer; therefore, for insurance against your bank failing, you would need to spread your cash among several institutions. Brokerage accounts insure your *ownership* of the securities up to a much higher level, normally up to 5 million. But of course, no one guarantees stocks and bonds against loss. The brokerage **money markets,** normally valued at $1.00 per share, are for your cash balances in a brokerage account, and are not covered under FDIC either; they are secured under SIPC (Securities Insurance Protection Corporation) which does not guarantee the value, but rather your ownership of the shares in the possibility the firm you're with goes bankrupt. In any event, money markets are generally thought to be the most conservative, backed by very short-term commercial paper (loans between corporations) and U.S. Treasury Bills.

If you have a big life insurance policy, you may need it. If you have young children and are the main breadwinner, and something happened to you, your income would likely need to be replaced. Or, you may have debt you wouldn't want your spouse to be saddled with after you're gone. But for someone who is retired, has a retirement account that covers your spouse, kids who are grown and doing well, don't have any debt to speak of, and have a high net worth, well, then you may not need that policy anymore. You might look into rolling the cash value into an investment or use it for income or in the future. Do seek professional help with this—more on this later.

You can consolidate these accounts making them easier to monitor. There are also costs associated with accounts like annual fees and management fees, so you could be paying more than your fair share here. If you have several small Individual Retirement accounts, IRAs, you can place them all with a mutual fund company, or, if you are very conservative, a bank IRA. We will delve into costs and asset placement in later chapters so you may not want to act on this yet. It's a good idea to have one or two checking accounts per entity, (one or two for you and your spouse, one for your business, etc.) One savings account, one or two IRAs each, and one or two non-retirement portfolios. We can't manage what we don't see and can't follow. Having a few big accounts focuses our attention on them! What you pay attention to GROWS. You are more likely to find time to open the statements and read them when you aren't looking at a paper mountain! (Not to mention the trees that will be saved! And even better to sign up for e-statements.)

You may even want to liquidate some of the very small accounts if they have been left unattended for years and don't show any progress. What if you have an old account that represents an old relationship in your life? If you look at it and feel your gut constrict or your body tightens up, that is one sign that you need to do something with that account—because it isn't doing anything for you except adding stress, and we are clearing stress too!

We can clean up costly debts and cut down on bills for things that don't support our growth, wellbeing, or fulfillment. For instance, are we spending money on bad habits, addictions? We can easily fall into lifestyles without even noticing how habit-forming certain behaviors can become. It can start out innocuously enough by allowing ourselves simple treats and other small indulgences. Before we know it, we have a bad habit that costs us our health and money, like smoking, drinking, eating out too often, and even splurging on distractions that are a cover for loneliness or some other lack inside. In finding new ways to save, we can really address so much more! We all have an inner knowing guiding us away from these things and when we are ready, they will fall away exposing more of our true, joyful selves.

Other pitfalls that are obstacles on the way to financial health are debts. Assess your biggest ones, your mortgage and your auto, student loans etc. If any one of these are causing you *pain,* keeping you up at night, or you're finding yourself not wanting to look or even think about them, it is time to take action to stop the pain. If more than 25% of your income is going to your mortgage payment, you are finding it hard to pay your bills, and you are worried sick, it's time to take stock. You might be hanging on to that house because you think it defines *who you are*. You may have allowed it to become part of your self-image. You are you, a complete, divine creature without those possessions! If you sell that house, (Please check with your tax advisor on the possible capital gains first) and get rid of that debt, you will feel *more* of who you are. You can always build toward having all of that along with peace of mind later, when you've manifested the life that supports it naturally. Start this process with good, comfortable feelings about your financial life now, and all will increase.

If you already have investments, you may have a *portfolio* (an account or accounts with securities — stocks, bonds, mutual funds, or exchange-traded funds (ETFs), or all of them). Find out what the costs are in the portfolio. There could be administrative costs, management costs, capital gains taxes, commissions, and income taxes. They can range from less than 1% to upwards of 3 or 4%. They could be creating a drag on the growth just like a car traveling with a flat tire. It is hard going to get anywhere. Also, by evaluating what you have, you can eliminate the poor performers, giving new life to your investments. But don't go too fast, this calls for more education and a meeting with a professional.

Different types of investments do better in different economic climates. This is called rotation, and you may have a high-quality mutual fund that goes down only to reflect its asset class. An *asset class* is a category of securities, for instance government bonds, or a group of large U.S. company stocks. These asset classes could represent over a thousand companies! As these asset classes rotate in turn, some are going up and some are going down as we go through different cycles. If you have too many in one type and it is going down, your entire portfolio is more at risk than you may be able to tolerate. There are proven methods to reduce risk and reduce cost.

This is financial housekeeping that should be done at least annually. Get a handle on the inherent costs of all your investments. Some *Wealth Coaches*[1] or *Registered Financial Advisor Representatives*[2] have access to information to give you an independent cost analysis of your portfolio. Be prepared, if you ask for a thorough diagnosis of the costs of your mutual funds, i.e. admin, management, commissions, fees, etc, you may be shocked to find out what you're paying. For instance, you are likely aware that there is trading going on in an actively traded mutual fund, but the costs of those trades are usually hidden.

Discovering all the various ways that negative ideas, financial worries, improper investment activities, and financial clutter that can put the brakes on our wealth formation gives us knowledge that moves

---

1 A Wealth Coach is someone who encourages you with inquiry and questioning to help you develop insight into your belief systems, monetary and otherwise. The Wealth or Financial Coach should have an extensive background in the financial world as well as coaching experience. A coach can help you gain clarity, help you find your true purpose, and simplify the complex world of finance. A Coach doesn't give you advice so much as helping you find your own goals, values and answers. The goal of a Coaching relationship is education, growth, raising awareness, and focusing on what *you* want, not what actions the expert would advise you to take. A coach helps *you* become independently aware and accountable. They work for a fee.

2 A Registered Investment Advisor representative is an independent advisor that may or may not manage money themselves. They either work for a fee or commission or both. It is not necessary for a RIA rep to be affiliated with a broker/dealer, but many are. Because they can work as a fee-based manager and fiduciary of your portfolio, they may be able to save you some costs. But you must be the detective here. A RIA will manage your portfolio, give you specific advice and direction, and needs to know your complete financial picture to give you recommendations. He or she is the one accountable and responsible.

us toward more wellbeing. We are clearing our way with as pure and positive a start as possible. Go ahead and get excited! Make sure your palms are open and not closed so you will be prepared to receive! You are learning when to use experts, what you can do on your own and most importantly, how you can create peace of mind when it comes to your financial future.

Read Every Morning and Evening Affirmation:

Those things that I desire are now in my focus. From a new and clear perception all that is left is abundant well-being supported by All That Is. All is well.

I relax into what I desire. I release any holding of that which no longer serves me. I release resistance to my good.

Chapter 2

Research

Who am I? What do I want?

"He who knows others is learned;
He who knows himself is wise."
– Lao-tzu, Tao te Ching

We assume we know who we are. When someone is asked about themselves—who they are, most of us will rattle off our position in a family, our occupation, where we live, and what we have. Yet this is just a fingertip of the grand scope of our identities. We are comprised of so many levels! Those of us who are earnestly working on finding our true selves, our gifts and passions, our reason for being here, are indeed fortunate.

Sometimes our close friends and family, a manager, a teacher, a counselor or coach, will give us insights into our strengths and talents that we hadn't recognized. For instance, as I already stated, while selling ad space to a brokerage office, I had no idea the manager would see something in me based on my ability to make a clear presentation to this potential client. He ended up offering me a job I hadn't even considered! (But I did indeed envision this *type* of career.)

Let's begin with a worksheet to learn more about ourselves when it comes to attitudes and money.

Now that you've looked at spiritual and physical wellbeing and connected it to financial wellbeing and have looked at how to begin addressing financial housekeeping, the next step is to look at what you can discover about yourself, what it is you want, what kind of person you are ... Use this worksheet as a tool to see how your understanding of attaining even better financial wellbeing has evolved. You may want to take out a pad of paper or open a new document to write down your answers. It's important to mindfully make connections to your past, your beliefs, and your present experience.

Worksheet Re-Scripting

Re-scripting: Eliminating obstacles and replacing them with fulfillment of your desires.

1. Where are you right now compared to your family of origin overall?

	Same	Worse	Better	Much Better
In lifestyle?	☐	☐	☐	☐
In wealth accumulation?	☐	☐	☐	☐
In ease of daily life?	☐	☐	☐	☐
In the feeling of power to control your circumstances?	☐	☐	☐	☐

2. Now, if you check any same or worse boxes, pause for a moment. Close your eyes, check in with your body, and just relax. Once you feel that calmness, look back on the list and stop on any SAME or WORSE checked box.We manifest from

our deep beliefs about life and they may be unconscious. This colors our thinking, choices and actions. Realize where you checked same or worse, you have the power to change if you so choose.

3. Who do you know, or know of, who represents to you the epitome of: (Write in the person(s) name in—may be several people: real, historical or fictitious.)

The greatest lifestyle _____

Wealth accumulation _____

Ease of living _____

Ability to fulfill his/her destiny _____

4. Focus on these people one at a time, imagining your life like theirs. See yourself moving through your day with their resources, support, ease and joy. Check in with your body and how it's responding – discomfort, comfort, twinges, aches, pleasant sensations, tightness, etc. With each vision, as you notice your bodies' responses (our thoughts and beliefs can tell us untruths but not our bodies) accept and allow these sensations. Embrace them, for they are important messages to you. Relax into them, and allow them to move through and eventually out of your body. By focusing on these role models, you get a taste, or a feel, for your ideal life that is palpable and more defined.

5. If you experienced discomfort in the previous exercise, realize that by denying or suppressing the feelings that came up, they won't get processed and released, and remain to return over and over again. The discomfort ultimately results in withholding love from yourself, judging yourself and lowering

your expectations. Write here what comes up now, whether you see patterns of self-sabotage, self-denial, feelings of unworthiness, etc.

_____

_____

_____

_____

_____

_____

_____

6. The higher version of you—your "Higher Self" or the Platinum Version of you, is calling you to grow, expand and stand for your unique truths. The beliefs and thoughts of the past are no longer useful. They may have kept you safe and feeling in control, but they also limited your present experience.

You are now waking up to new possibilities. You can summon the energy of the people in Number 3. This will enable you to break through previous barriers. When planning and taking action toward your goals, imagine what they would do, how they would do it and how they would feel.

Just as it is essential to research different types of mortgages, and what kinds of cars to buy, it is also essential to research the nature of reality and how it works. What laws seem to govern this thing called life? Are there any rules I need to know? Creating your life is the result of your decisions, attitudes, beliefs, and level of consciousness. Every evolutionary step on your path will bring new insights and rewards. It is the nature of reality to grow, expand and evolve.

Most importantly, the first thing to do is to begin the research of *who we are*—each one of us. Deepak Chopra, one of the world's most preeminent doctors of mind, body, spirit medicine, emphasizes that we ask this question of ourselves often. You may think you know yourself quite well, but hold on tight, you just might amaze yourself! Earnestly inquiring into what motivates you, what your true purpose is, what your basic assumptions are, and how you unconsciously react to events will give you the knowledge to generate your own growth, creativity, and evolution! This is a lifetime process, and one that can bring increasing dividends in the present; after all, who we really are is the eternal question. As we glean bits of the answer to this question, our lives become richer; we develop more understanding of our innate capabilities, and it will inevitably set us on a path full of wonder and awe.

Spiritually, *we will ask "Who am I?*
What do I desire?"

Physically, *we will ask "What have I created*
and why and where do I want to be?"

Financially, *"What are my financial goals?*
How can I stretch my ideas of numbers?

Spiritually, Who Am I? What Do I Desire?

Know thyself. Asking ourselves these questions can bring about insights that go to the foundation of our existence. Beneath our noisy ego we are, of course, anchored in spirit. Our spirit speaks to us in many ways; reflections in the material world, within the physical body, and in the realm of the mind. Spirit is in everything.

Each thought you have is creating an imprint in the unmanifest, or the *Field* if you will. Dr. David Hawkins, stated in his book, *Power vs. Force, The Hidden Determinates of Human Behavior*, "Every thought, action, decision, or feeling creates an eddy in the interlocking, interbalancing, ever-moving energy fields of life, leaving a permanent record for all of time. This realization can be intimidating when it first dawns on us, but it becomes a springboard for rapid evolution."

The more we ask these questions in a mindful way, the more we create space for greater awareness; and the more awareness we have, the happier we will become. Why? Because we will increasingly find, as Dr. Hawkins says in his book, *The Eye of the I*, "It was never the world that granted pleasure at all but one's own enjoyment of it." We have all heard such statements and we may sigh, "Oh, I know, I know"—yet we benefit from reaching a knowingness about it, a realization that reflects back to us who we really are.

Are we our thoughts, decisions, and actions? Are we our bodies, our brain, or our personality? Most people assume 'I am my body and my personality. I am a.... mother or a son or a husband or a boss or a teacher'.

Yet our body and our personality, our roles and our positions, are temporary. We have a wide range of potential; in fact, it would be accurate to say we are unlimited, for we are infinite. We originate from the source and we go back to the source, or field. Our spirit or energy is never extinguished, it just changes. And there is a purpose for our manifestation here; to find our purpose and serve it, giving us a sense of fulfillment and joy.

First let's look at our assumptions, beliefs and decisions from our ego's perspective right now. Our ego developed rapidly in the early years of our life, allowing us to make quick assessments of our surroundings and situations. These assessments further enabled us to come to certain conclusions about the world around us such as:

- Adult life looks hard
- The world will protect me
- Tomorrow will be better
- The future is scary
- There isn't enough (time, money, toys, love, fun etc.)
- Most people are nice
- The world is full of dangerous people
- The world holds lots of fun things to do

If we closely examine some of our conclusions, we can probably find that many of the 'facts' about the world we've picked up along the way vary greatly and may even contradict each other. The seed of doubt about the security that money can offer may have been planted when Mom repeatedly voiced her concerns about the lack of money. Dad may have spoken wide-eyed about a dream of making it BIG over and over

65

again until we realized eventually that it was only talk—and we decided it really was impossible for us because we never saw him actually follow his dream! The adults in our lives may have talked in very negative tones about the successful people they knew, labeling them with terms like greedy or arrogant, and we, without understanding envy, thought this must be true. And we grow up learning that maybe there isn't enough for everyone, that money isn't guaranteed and we may have to compete or fight and struggle our way to 'getting' what we want. (There actually is enough for everyone.)

Is the world a mostly dangerous place or a place full of wonderful possibilities? We are always building a case to support our opinions. That's why we like to listen to the political pundits with whom we agree! We are *always* gathering information to support our beliefs. In the throes of a political campaign, these beliefs get so entrenched that the supportive 'facts' get dug up, reframed, embellished, and inflated to a high-fevered pitch. We try to understand what is going on, but often we get the idea that there is only *one* right way to do something, and the other side is completely wrong. (This is the goal of the politicians!) Liberal activism and right-wing crusading are two different sides of the same coin. With spirit there are no opposites. There is no evil, and no hate. These concepts are created by the ego to explain misunderstood events, and they fit in nicely in a world of duality—good and bad, right and wrong, negative and positive. All judgments originate through the mechanism of the ego. From a spiritual perspective, all events springing up are part of creation, neither good nor bad, expressing endless forms and actions originating from beyond time and space. We so want to think that there is one 'right' and a definite 'wrong' but really there are endless ways of doing things. We get into problems when our ego gets attached to one way of doing things.

This, of course, carries over to our beliefs surrounding money and wealth; yours and others'. They are not facts. Find those moments in your past when you ingested a 'fact' about wealth. In your youth did someone take you to a fancy golf club or upscale restaurant and you felt out of place, with the reaction in your gut registering unease? Did you go play at a friend's house who had more than you, and the parents weren't warm to you, making you feel awkward in that environment? Even now, mentally seek the situations and places that may make you uncomfortable, those that you have a hard time seeing yourself in. Bring those images into the light and challenge them. Always remember, you are not your opinions. Know that you have the ability to change your judgments, thus changing your emotions, which will ultimately change your life. There are some experiments you can do right now and might be fun.

- Go test drive an expensive car.
- Imagine yourself in a job situation that you desire. See it in your mind's eye and feel it, notice your reactions to it.
- Look for open houses in your area. Find homes that you thought were out of your price range. Go see them. As you walk through these houses ask yourself why you can't live in one like this. Listen to your answers. Trace the answers to the belief.

Have fun with it. Approach it like a child's play. Then follow what ideas and thoughts come up for you. You may find yourself thinking that it's time to buy a house but are plagued with doubts: "Well I can't afford a house this expensive because my job doesn't pay enough." or "I couldn't get a mortgage." Now look at some possible reasons those doubts have crept into your thinking: "I'm stuck in a low paying job, I have to keep it because—1) I don't have the education to get a better one, 2) it's the only thing I know how to do…, etc."

Or maybe you would be more comfortable with looking at smaller, more affordable houses at this stage in your life. You may find that adjusting your expectations isn't that much of a compromise after all and you prefer a smaller house—that it suits you and you don't need more space. I'm not suggesting here that everyone has the same desires. Find what you desire and what your comfort level is and hang out with it a bit.

Here's an example that addresses how we flirt with our own desires but don't always think about acting on them; a young man loves airplanes. He could hang out all day at an airport looking at the planes, chatting with the pilots and the mechanics, and even paying for a ride in one of the private small planes. Then he asks himself why he isn't acting on his passion by taking up flying lessons. If we have a true passion it rises from our spirit, we should listen to that inner voice. It is telling us that this is where our joy lies and is a key to our purpose, or even how we can express our gifts and serve.

Part of the process of educating ourselves about who we are is to detach from the beliefs that are limiting us and replace them with beliefs that will ultimately allow us to be content. We are not limited. There is no reason we cannot have more joy and wonderment. Let's discover ways that we can change these beliefs and become open to a new perception of the world where our cherished desires find expression in our lives.

We all have moments in which we experience a Quantum Shift, resulting in a lasting change in perception. We make a decision based on new information or experience a new revelation that changes a root belief, and our life takes a dramatic turn. People faced with an emotional or physical crisis like a grave illness or physical danger sometimes change their whole life in an instant.

I had such an experience as a young Navy wife when my beloved husband received his orders to go to Viet Nam on an aircraft carrier. I knew the time would come for him to ship out, yet I hadn't faced it fully. (We never do.) Now pregnant with our first child, I felt I needed him, I couldn't do this without him, and he just could not go! It wasn't possible for me to go back to stay with my parents — they had their own problems. I thought that if we explained all this to the Navy Chaplain, he could help us (me). Maybe he would tell the Commander my husband needed to be home. I know it sounds crazy, but it was absolutely impossible for me to accept that he could leave me at that time!

So, we sat in the Chaplain's small, dark office as I softly cried. He looked at me with kindness and understanding in his eyes and said, "You will find out how strong a woman you really are." That's it. That's all he said. But I didn't feel angry or disappointed. Something deep inside me was struck. Deep down, I knew he was right. I had a quantum shift from the helpless girl to a strong woman *in that moment.* New energy patterns were created at the quantum level that gave me access to my own power that my beliefs had held at bay. That day I surrendered to what was. Fighting it was causing more suffering. I became committed to succeeding, to having our child on my own with courage, and to be cheerful in my many letters to my husband. How unfair it would have been had I sent my husband off with him thinking I would not be OK. It turned out that his parents were there for me and we became close, too.

It only takes a moment. Look back on your life and note when you made a decision or had a revelation that dramatically changed the course of your experience. It could have been a word from a teacher, boss, or parent; it could have been when you realized you had an ability or strength you hadn't recognized before, or it could have been an insight that rocked you so hard the world suddenly looked different. A quantum shift is actually a rise in consciousness, a widening of awareness, an increase in one's vibration, even if ever so slight. A small increase in consciousness can profoundly change the way you look at the world.

Ask yourself, Who Am I? What are my passions? We all have some developed skills and attributes, and others that are undeveloped, waiting in the wings to be called upon by a quantum shift. Our gifts are readily exposed when we are children. We naturally gravitate to what innately interests us. Some of our interests get smothered by our parents or society. How many of us are out there sitting behind a desk or behind a counter with no creative expression because our parents didn't see how our passions could make us money? What did you enjoy when you were twelve? Spend some time thinking about that because that may be a key for you if you are trying to find where your passions are. It may even answer Why You Are Here!

When bringing up our passions and our gifts I am reminded of an interesting post I saw by a very successful artist. While in high school he entered a painting in an art contest and won first place, and when that piece was entered in a contest for adults, it also won first place. He received a letter of congratulations from the principal and in it the principal said the student's development in this area was a great way to spend his later years and this hobby would be a good way to supplement his retirement income! I bet this accomplished painter is very happy he didn't listen to that adult!

As a senior in high school, I took the required aptitude test so the school guidance counselor could show me what direction to take in my education. She sat across from me with a perplexed look on her face. She said, "Kasey, you have scored extremely high on spatial relationships, and mechanics. I really don't know what to tell you. There isn't a path for a girl in this direction." What??? I was angry. I took two hours of art in an art class designed for students with an aptitude for it. Of course, the arts utilize this skill. Plus, what if I loved working on cars, or boats, or rocket ships? Thank God I didn't pay any attention to her words.

While looking back at your childhood it is also important to realize you have the imprint of your family history providing you with a pattern of experience that, without conscious awareness, you will inevitably repeat. If it is your goal to experience abundance and prosperity, you can, through your unique gifts, along with a quantum shift, create them. What does a prosperity attitude look and feel like? Do you feel your family might have lacked the ideal attitude toward prosperity, not just financially but perhaps spiritually, or in relationships, or life experiences? Sometimes a person searches their whole life for prosperity. Some people attain it intermittently, some do only once or twice, then lose it, and some never do. Then there are those who live in prosperity. You have probably heard the expression, prosperity consciousness. Prosperity consciousness is an attitude based on a belief in abundance. This belief in a plentiful world becomes a series of thoughts that are predominant in a person who *allows* abundance to flow.

Prosperity means different things to different people, but we are going to generalize here and say it is a feeling of ease unencumbered by the threat of any shortage. It is an underlying confidence—a trust that life will naturally provide what is needed when it is needed. This trust precedes any financial success. When our thoughts and feelings turn toward success repeatedly, patterns start to form and slowly gain momentum until they reach critical mass and are born into this material reality. First we simply put it out there and then we can surrender to the process. How the universe fulfills our desires may come in a different way than we ever could have imagined!

How do we change our thinking and behavior to allow the floodgates of abundance to open up in our lives? How do we change our beliefs so that we are filled with confidence that we are going to succeed? One moment at a time. It is overwhelming to think we must entirely overhaul the thought patterns that we've developed over our lifetime, but if we focus on what we can do right this minute—it isn't so hard to manage.

When you find a belief that is in opposition to abundance, and you start to pull that string to delete it, you may find it has wrapped itself into a knot of other similar beliefs. For instance, a belief that you aren't smart enough to be successful could be 'tied' to a belief that if you showed how smart you really were, it would have intimidated your father, making him angry, thus giving you another belief that showing your intelligence will get you into trouble. Or you may have a belief that rich people are socially irresponsible, but on following that thread, you find you believe that it is more meaningful for you to give than it is for a wealthy person, because they won't suffer or miss it, therefore, you are 'purer' by having less.

Observe your thoughts. Observe how they precede your feelings and emotions. Observe your physical reactions to those emotions, right now. Catch yourself when you say discouraging things to explain why you can't succeed, why it won't work; then sense how this feels as it bounces through your body—because it does. Every thought bathes your body in chemicals that can either invigorate you and your health or lessen your energy. Your higher-self has been waiting in quiet stillness for you to notice.

We've talked about beliefs and quantum shifts, and looked at our past to understand where our beliefs came from. Let's now look at 'What do I desire?'

You can make a list of possessions that you want to obtain, an income you would like to realize, a home or car you wish to own, and please do that. Then, however, I want to address the underlying meaning these will have for you. We can study book after book, acquire degree after degree, know a big number of facts to reach our goals, yet it is all insignificant without meaning. We probably all know people who have wealth in material things, yet they are downright miserable. They are always complaining that nothing ever seems to go right, they fuss over their purchases, worry incessantly about their investments, and seem to live without meaning in their lives.

By asking the deeper questions—by being still, we are creating an environment that quiets the ego long enough to let inspiration, insights, and intuition through. By being still we may invite a quantum shift. What are these messages saying? When we are inspired it is unmistakable, it gives us passion, joy, and energy and it serves the greater good in some way. Even if it is just raising your consciousness, it is benefiting the entire globe, for we are all one.

I recall a young man who left a 9 to 5 job to follow his passion which was to build beautiful hand-crafted wood furniture. It fulfilled him. Many people appreciated his fine craftsmanship, and he was able to support his family well with it. What would give meaning and purpose to your life?

Dr. David Hawkins, in his book '*The Eye of the I,*' discusses meaning in our lives. He wrote, "It is meaning that empowers and transforms people's lives, and the only importance of facts is what they actually mean to them. Meaning arises from value. Joy does not come from figures or statistics but from what they mean."

What facts about you and your life give you meaning? Maybe you have a secret talent you want to share—what equity do you have in you to spend in the world? What gives you joy? Maybe taking care of your family is where you find meaning and you want to feel abundant there. Or possibly you have a drive to explore, learn, and then teach what you've discovered. What drives you today? Do you feel moved to be a healer in some capacity? So many occupations encompass healing such as counseling, massage, life coach, etc.—it doesn't have to mean doctor or nurse. In fact, once I felt a headache coming on just before my hair appointment with a new hairdresser. After spending one hour in her care, my headache was gone and my body was restored and at ease. It was her healing touch I am sure—she is a healer and I wonder if she even knows!

The archetype of teacher is expressed in myriad ways as well—many wise people tell wonderful stories with underlying lessons. When we find our passions and act on them, we are aligned with God's will—we are in harmony with the universe. There will be a peace and ease associated with it. We will have meaning and a sense of well-being.

Let's tease out more answers with an exercise that's worked for so many.

List 25 answers to the question 'What do I desire?'

Write beside each one the meaning or value it would bring. First, get still, breathe slowly and calmly. Don't think too much about it. Go with stream of consciousness. For example: I desire marriage to share love, or I desire a career using my creative talents so I might give joy to others. Read these each morning upon arising and each night before going to sleep. Meditate or pray asking what your purpose is. What are you here to do? What makes you different from others? Whom do you want to emulate? Who do you admire, living or dead, real or mythological? When are you the most satisfied?

Physically we ask, *"What have I created and why? Where do I want to be?"*

We can examine the distance between what we want and what we have. Sometimes we unconsciously throw obstacles in our way when seeking something. We could even fear what we desire—remember opposing beliefs, *i.e.*, money is good, rich people are bad? Or perhaps we feel we are unworthy.

This is a good time to examine one of the most pervasive, destructive emotions human beings suffer from, and that is guilt. And we continually manifest it on our own. Sometimes guilt exists on autopilot, slowly paralyzing us, seemingly coming out of nowhere catching us in an unguarded moment bringing us down. It doesn't discriminate and hits us all. Without the tools to recognize it and override it, guilt can have enormous control over our lives. More self harm has been wrought from our feelings of guilt and regret than any other. Guilt can freeze us in our tracks, suppress our goodness and joy, and make us feel unlovable, fearful, unworthy, prevent our success, and always be in the background ready to lash at us evermore. If we don't address our guilt, we can go on punishing ourselves endlessly.

I want to assure you that any guilt we carry is a collective, ego-induced falsehood. Every one of us has made errors in our past which we profoundly regret. We label them on a scale of small to large, yet they are all insidious, lying in wait to surface when we are most vulnerable. The human experience is something we all have in common, and we all share in our own perceived wrongdoings. By the very nature of being human and operating from the ego, we all share in the error of believing in a dualistic world, a world of black and white, right and wrong. As our consciousness expands our understanding of 'right and wrong' beliefs, actions, and feelings change. A good psychologist friend once told me that 'at every moment we are doing our best with the information we have at the time.' You've probably had times where you've said or done something out of fear, anger, or shock that you would label as horrible. Whatever you have done it was because:

1) You were operating from the very limiting ego.

2) The collective ego of humanity was the source.

3) It originated from the survival patterns of the animal world.

I refer once again to Dr. Hawkins because he covers this so succinctly in his book, *I, Reality and Subjectivity*, "Even education is dedicated primarily to survival and success. The inherent motives of the ego are therefore survival and gain, of which both are fear-based." Hawkins explains how we now use our intellect, which evolved into an important tool for survival, for elaboration of what are basically animal instincts. In other words, operating from our humanness, we are still driven by our animal nature, still driven to survival and gain; but as we act on these impulses our intellect labels and punishes us! Knowing this gives us the ability to forgive others and ourselves. Dr. Hawkins states, "Relief of guilt and greater compassion for oneself and others occurs through realizing that the individual person did not volitionally create the structure of the ego, nor did anybody else."

Through forgiveness of self and others, we can progress on our path to transcend the ego and its consequent suffering. This is immensely important. Forgiving ourselves for any past harm we have caused ourselves and others is essential for our growth and for realizing our own happiness.

The media and our culture are complicit in supporting this myth of guilt. We are repeatedly told we're 'supposed' to feel great guilt in order to be a 'good' person. I am not talking about denying having done something wrong; we can admit it, atone and accept the consequences, learn from the experience, apologize from the heart, but then, get back to compassion and love for ourselves and others.

Actually, we also tend to confuse guilt with other emotions like disappointment, sadness, regret, and fear that we did something wrong. Ask yourself if you did anything immoral or illegal. Probably not.

The past mistakes and harm we have caused others likely took place when our ego was threatened, our fear and anger took over and we didn't have the awareness to control it at the time. Something mean was said, an action that hurt others, or assistance was withheld. We've all been there.

Feel regret but then allow it to dissipate. Our hurts, traumas, and bad experiences are held energetically within our bodies ready to resurface when our 'buttons' are pushed and subside only when we are ready to sit quietly and allow the pain to be felt and released. Great books are written on this very subject, all pointing to ways to let go. There is a list of recommended books on the site; https://kaseyclaytor.com/reading/ (see resources, recommended reading, under *Dealing with "Dark Nights of the Soul"*).

We also could be harboring grievances that weigh us down. Inside every grievance is the seed of transcendence; opportunities to gain insights that will free up positive movement into a more miraculous existence. In *A Course in Miracles,* it suggests, "Perhaps it is not yet quite clear to you that each decision that you make is one between a grievance and a miracle, (ACIM, W-78.1:1-4)". The ego is always looking for ways in which to be offended! Watch your 'self' during the day—how many times do you get bent out of shape for things like someone cutting in front of you in line, or someone failing to follow through on something you wanted them to do? Or someone just doing something differently than you would have!

The *Universal Forgiveness Treatment* by Catherine Ponder, of Unity Church Worldwide, was shared with me years ago by a young man who said it changed his life. Upon meditatively repeating it, he suddenly experienced a physical sensation of a dark heaviness lifting out of his body and floating away. It was such a moving experience he fell to the floor in a heap of tears. You can google it for yourself.

Guilt and forgiveness are intertwined with our relationship to financial health by eclipsing our view of what can be. If we can't even entertain the possibility of a deeply held dream because we deem ourselves too flawed or unworthy, how can we move forward? Learning about how these two states impact our lives provides an opportunity to finally release the guilt and forgive ourselves. Learning about ourselves with compassion opens new possibilities.

Where do you want to be?

When we remember a time in our life, not only do we remember the visual sense of it, but it comes with a mood, predominant colors, or scents. A rainy day could bring back a memory of walking to grade school in the showers, everything grey and wet, smelling like earthworms and steaming asphalt, or a memory of the movie theatre with its greasy popcorn and soda smells and bright colors on the screen.

While doing the following exercise imagine as many of your senses as possible to make it more impactful. Remember shifting your mindset to more success in all areas will naturally result in more financial rewards down the road.

Exercise:

When you think of where you want to be—identify 1) Your mood, 2) the environment, 3) the colors, 4) the expectations, and 5) the consequent effects. For example, let's say you want to become an awesome speaker, this desire has meaning and great value for you, and you want the opportunity to share your knowledge this way. In your mind's eye not only will you see yourself giving an articulate well-delivered talk, but you will also bring the intention to feel confident, competent, and grateful. The colors you see around you will be uplifting colors. The audience is eagerly anticipating your next sentence, and finally, you are reaping the financial rewards of your talents. Visualization works to bring about our desired manifestations if combined with the feelings or essence we intend the results to create. Our experiences are all multileveled—spiritual, physical, and emotional, and it's most effective to cover all three. That is why gratitude is included, because if what you desire is aligned with what is best for your growth, you have a reason to be thankful.

Personal growth that comes with knowing yourself leads to better decisions toward wellbeing.

Daydream. Pretend. It's almost a lost art but is an important part of creating a fulfilling life. Children naturally daydream given some unscheduled time. When they act out their daydreams, we call it play and pretend. It is of the utmost importance to give children free time and space to just be. Their time will always be well spent, even though it looks to us like they are goofing around and doing nothing in particular. In their daydreams they try on different roles, imagine different stories played out with themselves as hero, victim, bystander, or all three! Do you remember great stories played out in your head as a child? We all love 'A Christmas Story,' in part because we all remember those great daydreams of what we could do or how we could get our parents' undivided attention or save the day!

Seriously, daydreaming is an important component to the self-actualizing adult. If you are to create the life of your dreams, you need to withdraw from worldly concerns to allow your imagination to roam where it will. Set aside a day off where you just lounge around with no agenda. Take a walk; drink in nature, try to have solitude and journal. Try some of the ideas in books like Julia Cameron's 'The Right to Write' to get your creativity jump-started. You will discover ideas will pop up one after another. This will help you develop your ability to create what you intend and even foster a Quantum Shift.

Where are you right now? Let's allow ourselves to slip into the abstract. Before you experience anything in your reality, there is first the Unmanifest. All potentiality for forms, experiences, events, emotions, thoughts, and actions lies in the quantum level only to be pulled into manifestation by our perpetual act of creating!

In the 1970's, scientist Helmut Schmidt invented a machine that was designed to randomly click in the right or left ear of the experimenter. He proved scientifically that through intention, the subject' could change the randomness of the pattern and influence the clicks to happen more in one ear than the other. The intention of the subjects happened by choosing which ear they preferred the hear the clicks in. It did indeed prove intention affected the clicks. Even more startling were the results of a test when the taped results were sent home with one of the influencers. The effect on the tape was a change in the original output of the machine! Intentions can act on probabilities whether in the past or in the present! Intentions determine what events actually come into being!

We all have desire; it flows up through us as naturally as breathing. Inherent in desire is an attachment to results, future thinking, noticing an absence in the present, and maybe even a 'grasping'.

Intention is a present energy, right here, right now. With intention comes powerful manifestation. When we hold an intention together with a desire and know how we would like the end result to look, yet allow the manifestation to happen without our interference, (our insistence that it unfold a certain way) it cannot help but come to fruition. Quite possibly the outcome may manifest itself in a different, even more glorious form than we could have ever imagined.

Set an intention, cradle it within a Sacred Container, embrace uncertainty, and let it go. It is your job to do what is before you that is giving you inspiration, passion, and joy. It is not your job to resist what is. What is — is perfect.

When you wake up in the morning there is a gradual, gentle organizing within your awareness of the new day. You may feel neutral at first, or peaceful. Maybe you start thinking about what you need to do right away. But there is always a coloring of that day in your psyche as you wake up. Do you wake up with dread? Something impending? A loose, carefree feeling? We all have different types of days. If grievances steal their way into our minds, or we place too much expectation on ourselves, the colors for that day will be murky. To get an idea of what I mean, think back to a very unpleasant experience you had. There will be a thick, almost tangible mood that is translated from sounds, colors, and emotions. These are usually the first forms pulled forth from the Unmanifest and mass consciousness. They eventually coalesce into words in our mind that we associate with those feelings. In recalling different times in your life, you can probably associate eras of these gatherings of pre-thoughts; a time in your life that you experienced lack, poverty or illness, or joy, abundance, and optimism.

Where are you now? What are you attracting into your reality? How light or heavy is your life now? You can attract a gentle, peaceful existence, or a dynamic, robust one. Reach within, and all worlds are possible.

Financially, "What are my financial goals? How can I stretch my ideas of numbers?"

There are three main types of people when we examine financial behavior. There is the saver; when money flows to these folks they tend to hold on to it, taking some out of circulation. They feel more comfortable letting it build up at the bank but begin to sweat when a reason for a big expense presents itself. These people are usually responsible, dependable, and financially conservative. They sometimes have a hard time placing money in investments. If this type gets out of balance, they could suffer from stagnation, hoarding, or apathy in creating their own financial plan. (By 'out of balance' I mean leaning toward an unhealthy extreme, due to unchecked emotional problems and/or erroneous thinking. This is how all of us get out of balance).

The second type is the spender - impulsive, great fun, but not a habitual saver. They are distractable and may be unable to follow a disciplined path. Because this type is often in the red, they may not have enough reserves which would make them vulnerable to financial crises.

The third type is the controller. They don't have a problem saving or spending, especially after they have done their homework, know their goals, and have a plan. The danger of the extreme here is over-managing, over-researching, and not leaving investments alone long enough to bear fruit. Sometimes the controller can't make a decision because of constant second guessing, worrying the research didn't go deep enough, or that they missed a better investment.

Most people are a combination of these, but usually one is dominant. If you know yourself well and you know where your tendencies are, you can compensate for them. Learning how to begin bringing yourself more into balance in all areas of your life is essential. Finding a good Financial Coach can help with this specifically. Your plan for your financial future needs to have built-in safeguards to keep you out of trouble. On our path toward abundance, it is helpful to define what abundance means to us financially, what steps we can take to stay on the path before we ultimately attain it.

How much is enough? If you ask someone worth one million dollars what amount would make them feel they have enough, I'll bet they will say 2 or 4 million. Ask someone who has 5 million; she will probably say 8 or 10 million. Everyone wants more money. What's going on here? Is it our natural drive to always want more? Our mental operating system, our ego, combined with our emotions, is never satisfied. The ego is continually analyzing the landscape of our environment buying into messages that tell us what we must have, building habits that only satisfy us temporarily. We all realize at some point that we get trapped in a cycle of desire, attainment, happiness, and then dissatisfaction again. We get used to a raise in income or new purchases, until our desires fire up again, and it doesn't take long. We get the new furniture, then in a little while we look around to see what we want next! Fulfilling desires is fun; a very creative act, and no doubt it will continue until we leave this world. At the same time, we can find a deeper, more constant sense of joy underlying our life no matter what the outward circumstances may be. How to fulfill your desire and also find joy are both important concepts to keep in mind.

The emphasis here is to start at a level deeper than the constant drives of the ego. Create the lifestyle you dream of now with small changes. Your actions, words, and behavior need to be aligned with success. It doesn't happen until they are. I don't mean spend money you don't have or take a trip you can't yet afford; I am talking about attitude. Care for what you *do* have, appreciate it, for what you pay attention to grows. If you have $2,000 to invest, do it mindfully, with care. You are preparing and educating yourself to handle more money. It is common for people who win the lottery to be broke within a couple of years. Why is this? Well, in part, because handling money is a learned skill. Part of that skill is discipline. Here again, a Wealth or Financial Coach can help educate you and inspire you to raise your awareness in this area. Care about yourself and your profession with the intention to succeed. Take care of your wardrobe, your car, and your furnishings as if they were priceless! This helps bring you into alignment with what you desire. You attract what you resonate with.

You may dream that you want 2 million dollars and then you will relax, then you will be happy. Having that amount is fine, but working from the standpoint of lifestyle will more likely bring you the satisfaction you are looking for. The money will appear to support that lifestyle, because what we choose to believe and then act on will change all aspects of our lives.

I have a couple who have been clients of mine for 17 years. They are a perfect example of what I'm talking about. When their kids grew up, they had many discussions about how and when they would retire. They wanted to retire in their 50's! As a financial planner it was my job to tell them how much MORE money they would have if they kept working until the typical retirement age of 65 or later. This couple is very creative in choosing lifestyle over some set amount of money. They both have strong passions; crafts, traveling, operating small, undemanding businesses and the like. Against my 'educated' advice they retired about 6 years ago. They are flourishing. They own two homes, an RV, and are tickled pink with their life. If their only goal was a set amount of money, they would still be working at jobs they were miserable in! They concentrated on a lifestyle choice and the lifestyle manifested! They saw their ideal and stepped into it. One thing they did before retirement was to accelerate their mortgage payments to pay off their house. They put in energy to seeing their dream through. I know they weren't always completely confident it was going to work, but hey, they were young enough to go back to work if they had to.

If you concentrate on what would be a fulfilling life for you, one with purpose and meaning, ideas will come. Read books that inspire you, dream, and act as if your life is like that right now. And if you put a number on your goal for financial worth, isn't that limiting you? This is where you can stretch your ideas of numbers.

If you are old enough you can relate to this — remember as a young adult how much you made? And as your salary grew, you grew into the salary? At first you were so excited when you received a big increase in income, but then you adjusted to it until it didn't seem like so much. All the things you buy have gone up over the years; probably you can buy better quality now. Think of how $100.00 has changed in your mind. It is almost like that amount of spending energy is easier and easier to attain. Why not $1,000.00? Expand what you think of as an average easy amount to attain. Get used to the feel of $1,000.00 as a very comfortable, small amount of money. Then raise it!

I noticed this working for me as a young broker. What I had thought of as a large amount of money kept rising, and what I thought of as an easy amount to earn went up as well. Look up, build momentum and your life is one of endless possibilities. If you want two million dollars yet in your gut you don't really believe that would be possible, start with a more reasonable amount for you and when it feels comfortable and possible, go up a little.

We need practical tips for where we place our money, using care and attention. Here are some sound guidelines to get you in good financial shape.

- **A good rule of thumb is to keep three to six months of expenses in an emergency fund**. This could be a savings account or a money market, somewhere that you can access the money easily. If you have a tendency to spend what you see in the bank, invest in a mutual fund money market without checking. It will be a little harder to spend it when your impulses are kicking in. If you don't have that much right now, start with what you have and pay into that account monthly just like it is another fixed expense. Pay yourself first.

- **Own your home**. This is an important building block for most people and it is probably the biggest investment for many. It is a solid foundation on which to grow. Invest some time into researching qualifications, and you can talk with mortgage lenders.

- **Invest in real-estate if you have an inclination towards it**. Find a mentor or coach who has expertise in this area to help you navigate this venture. You may have a knack for it.

- **Invest in Securities.** If you neither have the time nor talent for, nor the inclinations to have a hands-on go with real-estate, this is a wonderful opportunity. It is also much more liquid.

- **Add regularly to a retirement account.** If it's with your company great! They often match what you put in. If not, start your own or have both if you qualify.

If you already have an investment portfolio:

- **Find a good Wealth Coach or Registered Financial Advisor** and have them do an analysis of your portfolio to determine the costs, both declared and hidden.

- **Have your account measured for risk.** That will tell you the range of volatility inherent in it. That means how much it could potentially go up in a bull market and how much it might go down in a bear market.

- **Have your account measured for diversification**. You may have 10 mutual funds and still be too undiversified because of duplication in the funds, and the stocks in the mutual funds could represent a very small piece of the market.

Affirmations on Research:

I am learning more everyday about who I really am.
My inner being is surprising me with new creativity and new ideas to move me toward my desires.
I joyfully accept all the goodness that flows to me, materially, spiritually, and financially.

Chapter 3

Cycles

Flowing Into the Rhythms of Nature

"Adopt the pace of nature: her secret is patience."
– Ralph Waldo Emerson

Even our system of commerce, supply and demand, and the investment markets follow cycles explained in this chapter. Everything in the world is in a rhythm, waxing and waning in a steady tempo that we are subject to. If we fight these movements our progress is hampered. When we learn to detect these cycles in and around us, we have an advantage, we can step into the beat, flow into the energy and feel less resistance to accomplish our desires. As sure as the sun rises each day, water rains and evaporates, seasons fold into one another, and our bodies rotate through the endless number of processes to keep us alive, we can forever count on change; life is always in a state of flux. 'Everything in its proper time', 'let nature take its course', 'there is a time for everything', and 'for every time there is a season'. These are all little jewels of wisdom we grew up hearing, yet in the busy working day, getting children off to school, rushing to work, hurrying home to prepare dinner — we ignore the beat pulsing under life; it gets drowned out. In our harried world we forget that our physical bodies are of the world and are affected by the movements of nature's cycles. Even our digestion changes with the time of day. You will see how this cycling matters within our perception of time. That no matter how impatient we are, things only happen 'in their due time.' If we push past the natural speed (nature's speed) we become forgetful, accident prone, ignoring signs and cues, and stay on the surface of life.

My son illustrated this point while surfing. There was a hurricane offshore, not threatening us on the East Coast, but churning up big powerful waves. Anyone who's ever cared about surfing will head to the beach on such days, big waves being so rare here. When a wave is big and powerful you better go with it once you catch it. My son caught a huge one, road it to the crest, and in his impatience, made the fatal mistake of turning against the direction of the wave too early, with one slight leaning. He and the board tumbled down the face of the wave, rolling over and over. The fin of the surfboard struck his elbow while he was churning under water which resulted in his need to drive himself to the hospital for stitches. Had he been mindfully moving with the wave his body would have synchronized automatically, all fine motor movements in tune, giving him a flawless ride.

Spiritually, we will ask "What are cycles of the universe? How does that affect us?"

Physically, we will ask "How can we become in sync physically and materially to improve our lives?"

Financially, we will ask "What are the economic and stock market cycles and how can we take advantage of them?"

***Spiritually**, "What are cycles of the universe? How does that affect us?"*

Cycles of the Universe

In the Infinite Field there is a cycle of energy. Underlying physical manifestation there is the Unmanifest and the dance between the two. At the subatomic level, physical forms pop in and out of existence, alternating between waves of energy and quantum particles. Astrophysicists call this field the Zero Point Field and some believe that this field of unimaginably large quantum energy in so-called empty space could be harnessed to give us an inexhaustible source of power! Furthermore, if we are all invisibly connected to everything else through this Field, in this invisible matrix of energy, it would then make sense that this Field would be encoded with information, a memory if you will, of the universe. And we are always in touch with it, information flowing to and from us, events percolating up out of nowhere, with no apparent causality, yet all in perfectly ordered chaos, like a sudden summer shower on a sunny day.

And this energy translates or manifests as a vibration. Throughout the day you are living in a matrix of vibrations—you also resonate with the vibration that initiates and makes possible the events and surroundings in your reality. You attract the people, places and things that inhabit your environment through the culmination of your Karmic values and evolution of consciousness, or your vibration.

This cycle is the flow of creation—from the unmanifest, the stillness, the silence containing all the imaginable and unimaginable, the mind of God, as Deepak Chopra says, to the perpetual act of creating. And every one of us is doing this every moment of every day. This is the mother of all cycles. What a loose and watery place this is until we step back away from it as the observer—and how hard for our ego to define as reality slips away under our fingers when we try to pin it down!

Ancient texts tell us we are bound by the law of Karma, the Bible tells us that what you sow you shall reap, and in modern times we say what goes around, comes around, you get what's coming to you. Beyond the material world, in the Infinite Field, there is an organizing power that rights all action, balancing and resolving, so that every thought and deed is rectified.

Every spiritual tradition teaches lessons relating to the results of one's actions. It is a divine and perfect system. No ultimate punishment is required because all of our thoughts and actions register our experiences within our psyche and soul. This is impressed upon the Field, and the results of that manifest in the material world, creating this ongoing experience we call life. Our intentions, expectations, and desires are all sent into the universe, God. What we want, our desire and what we visualize for ourselves is telegraphed in a continuous moment by moment vibration. What we put out, give, display, produce, create, exude, feel, all eventually comes back to us in some form or manner that is equal to what was sent forth. This is the cycle of Spirit with the unspoken eventuality of Enlightenment, Unity, Oneness. It becomes difficult here to separate Spirit and the material world, for there is only one Reality, all ultimately is Spirit. From the enlightened ones we learn that at the point of oneness all duality—cause and effect, good and bad, past and future, right and wrong—ceases. Everything is seen as one. But for the rest of us, we continue with our ego shaded glasses wondering what will happen next and why. As we grow in consciousness, we may notice more coincidences. As events cycle by us we may notice patterns. And if we aren't paying close attention to worldly things, we may notice these coincidences falling right in front of us, from the simple everyday coincidences like the appearance of an item we had just realized we needed, the phone call from someone we intended to contact, to the realization of an experience we had desired as if it was attracted to us like a magnet!

Give that which you want to receive. If you want abundance in your life, in all areas, look for openings to give; a smile to someone having a bad day, an anonymous gift of a meal for a family on hard times, helping round up the lost animals after a terrible storm, or teaching others a skill. There are as many ways to give as there are human beings. This is purposefully taking part in the movement of the universe. This, also, is where it benefits us to know ourselves well, so we can utilize our gifts. Develop virtuous behavior. The result from using these gifts for the betterment of humanity is goodness multiplied.

Notice when you may be feeling sorry for yourself, thinking you are in such a difficult situation that you just feel like giving up. At the same time, someone in need crosses your mind or you see or hear of them. As soon as you consider doing something for them, voila! you begin to shift your emotional tide in the other direction. Energy is coming back to you now. Karma. When you act you are changing the patterns from your very essence.

To further our progress, we learn in the *Bhagavad-Gita*[1] to act — without being attached to results. This reminds me of a rather grouchy client I had many years ago. It seemed I was always doing an enormous amount of extra work for her! She was never satisfied. I was going beyond my normal services for her. And I kept waiting for her to appreciate it! And she didn't! She expected it. I was looking for *thank-yous,* and I was attached to that possible outcome. I even chose to feel offended. Oh, how our ego loves to find a reason to feel offended! The lesson I finally learned was this — when you do something for someone, do it with the intention that the act itself is complete, the act is the sole purpose. The act can be a divine offering. Actually, all actions can be so offered.

I remember reading a book on the life of St. Frances of Assisi that told of his dedication to God with every act he performed and every word he uttered. Good deeds are their own reward in and of themselves. As for the grouchy woman, once I gave up the attachment to hearing her say thank you, it was easier for me to be more reasonable and limit my 'extra' work for her. Going even further with this example, I can look back and see how I was becoming grouchy because I was resentful! Act without being attached to results.

The cycle brought on by attachment is familiar to us when thinking about desire. We yearn, attain, experience happiness, and then it starts over again. But we also get attached to self-punishment through guilt, anger, and resentment. Some of us inflict internal verbal assaults which give us the message we are not enough. The results of this cycle

---

1 An ancient text from India written in the form of a poem that tells the story of a young warrior who finds the god, Vishnu, as the personality Krishna, in his chariot before battle.

are stress, headaches, fatigue, pain and more. Some of us are harder on ourselves than we would ever be on our friends and family.

We work hard but it isn't good enough. We blame ourselves for events that don't go how we think they should. We take responsibility for others' feelings. We may not even be aware of the self-inflicted reprimands stealthily sneaking into our thoughts every day. "Oh, I could have handled that better." "That mistake was so stupid!" "If only I had more education, I would be more respectable." "He is so much smarter than me." "Oh, that was so dumb." "I should work harder." "I shouldn't have gotten mad." Or my personal favorite, "Now why did I say THAT?"

To release ourselves from this cycle we can gently notice doing this and realize it is a choice. We can welcome in self-appreciation and love. This is true freedom. One exercise for this is to sit quietly by yourself and direct all the love you have for all things and people back to yourself. With gratitude and wonder fill yourself with all the tenderness, helpfulness, and kindness that you would reserve for the most cherished ones in your life. Declare a *Day of Freedom* and come back to this over and over throughout your day. We can drive ourselves so hard. We seem to be telling ourselves what we do is never enough. We must do more. On your *Day of Freedom* choose to see yourself as a child of God on a divine appointment.

On my own spiritual path, I know the inspirations and messages from my inner being are those adoring, encouraging and absolutely loving ones. There is no judgment, no possibility of wrongness, just lovingness, total acceptance and support. Any messages you receive that aren't in your highest good are from your ego.

Another cycle worth mentioning here is what I call the 'start over'. Remember when you were a child in school forming letters on a piece of paper? Perhaps you experienced frustration because you kept making mistakes. You would erase or cross out the imperfect letters until your paper was a mess and the teacher came over with a crisp clean new piece of paper saying those joyful words, "You can start over." Every day we can start over. We always have start-overs! Mary Pickford said, "You may have a fresh start any moment you choose, for this thing that we call 'failure' is not the falling down, but the staying down."

There are the 'start-overs' of young animals in nature. We have ospreys living around us and I watch the new fledglings with fascination each spring. Last year there were three hatchlings in close proximity to our dock on a river. One had a particularly difficult time learning to fly, catch fish, and just about everything else she had to learn. It was with a mix of humor and pain that we watched her lessons.

As we began a walk along the river one morning all the young ospreys were gliding over the water scanning for fish. Upon our return we saw a female coming in for a landing on the dock railing, where her two siblings were. She came in way too fast. She tried and failed to grab the railing with her feet, but with her great momentum she stumbled onto the dock, then into the water! She flapped around awkwardly for what seemed like several minutes before she finally, finally broke free of the water and took to the air again. She circled, eyed the dock, and made another attempt. This time she landed on the dock, but again she had too much momentum and spilled into the water. We watched helplessly as she became waterlogged and I was sure she was the one who wouldn't make it. Yet she kept trying. She eventually perched by her siblings on the railing. They all learned to fly, land, fish, and survive. Start-overs are a natural part of life. In the animal world it is taken for granted. They don't have a choice to 'give up'. What can you start-over in your life?

On our path we can get discouraged, even full of anguish. I was in such a state about a dear project when my assistant, Dawn, reminded me to just look at how far we've come, instead of that expanse out in front of us between where we are now and where we want to be. There is truth in that. Looking at that unknown expanse with fear may create resistance to our personal growth.

If you get discouraged or anxious, look at how many of your dreams have come true. Upon reaching a particular desire, it's natural to relish it for a moment before you begin building upon another desire. We are always somewhere in this cycle. Pause in your **now** and allow the gratitude of what you've accomplished to sink in, acknowledging the gifts acquired on your path.

From our perspective, our exalted teachers look like they have found a state of constant enlightenment, while we still have fits and starts, times of doubts and self-recrimination. Yet those sages also experience the pain of growth. If you've received a calling, a passion to grow in a certain direction, it is not an even, linear path! It is more like a spiral. It's similar to driving down the highway and passing a long group of slower moving cars. Eventually you break free of the group. Now you are out front on your own section of highway flying free and feeling good. What happens next? In due course you encounter the next group and once again, you are at the back of the line. (i.e.: desire, growth, attainment, desire). Once you make a decision to follow your own path, you will find the challenges that go with it.

Eckhart Tolle, Dr. David Hawkins, Michael Singer, Byron Katie, and many, many others have written about the anguish of the soul during the growth cycle. In fact, Jack Kornfield, a well-known author, master meditation teacher and a trained Buddhist monk for 30 years, wrote a book on this subject, '*After the Ecstasy, the Laundry, How the Heart Grows Wise on the Spiritual Path*'.

If you plunge through that portal of difficulty on your path, and it seems as though you've fallen back to the end of the line, look behind you. Look how far you've come. Make it easier on yourself. Honor yourself with the same compassion that you have for your most cherished friends. It will pass, it is normal, and you are OK.

The universe is a symphony of energetic cycles; our lives are full of giving and receiving, experiences cycling in and out of our physical existence. We experience cycles in groups also, through mass consciousness, a result of the sum total of the group's vibration.

> ***Physically***, *"How can we become in sync physically and materially to improve our lives?"*

The physical world and all its inhabitants, being subject to space and time, are in an eternal dance of change. We are born, grow, age, and die. The earth revolves around the sun as it slowly turns on its axis giving us the days and years. It wobbles a bit on that axis giving us the seasons. Our physical bodies are not only intimate with the earthly cycles but are of them. The cycles of the physical universe and our planet Earth are fairly obvious but our connections to them are more subtle.

We are discovering some before unknown conditions as a result of ignoring our relationship to the cycles of nature. Depressive episodes brought on by the lack of periodic exposure to the sun or ignoring our need for rest during the night are common examples of this. Health problems often arise when people change work shifts from day to night and back again. Even our exposure to the glow of our devices before bed can cause our sleep cycle to be interrupted. Our physiology changes with the stimulation brought on by the content of the images and stories.

A report on sleep stated that the average sleep time for people before the electric light bulb was invented was 10 hours per night! Getting a good night's sleep every night will boost your immune system, help you stay clear headed, and improve your memory, helping you live your life with the enthusiasm that you were designed to have. We evolved to follow the cycles of the moon and the sun, not a clock.

To a large degree, we've also lost the natural rhythm of our digestive system, not waiting for cues of hunger and fullness to direct our eating. We eat, drink, and sleep from daily habits, visual cues, convenience, and opportunity. Within our physical selves an innate intelligence is always communicating to us where the body is within its many cycles. Part of an abundant life is making choices that support the body in balancing itself toward abundant health! The medical term for this is called homeostasis, the ability or tendency of an organism to maintain internal equilibrium by adjusting its physiological processes. There are many complex biological mechanisms that operate via the autonomic nervous system to offset disruptive changes, balancing such things as blood pressure, body temperature, PH of blood, hormone levels, etc. We can see how this system is integral to maintaining health and vitality. This process even extends to our psychological balance, always seeking to compensate for stress, depression, anger, with the succession of chemicals and hormones released into our bodies in response. To invite abundance into our lives we can create a culture of balance within our physiology. When we feel refreshed, rested, with a clear mind, we can more easily achieve whatever will fulfill us!

One of the most impressive life sciences that I have ever studied is Ayurveda. Ayurveda is believed by many to be the oldest healing system in the world; it dates back thousands of years in India. Ayurvedic physicians believe food has medicinal properties, all disease begins when we are out of balance, and a patient given the right foods and herbs, etc. to eat and drink along with physical practices, will be brought into balance. They also believe there are beneficial times to eat and a time to rest the digestive track. If we watched a person living an 'Ayurvedic' lifestyle we would see someone living in tune with his or her body, being aware of any symptoms of imbalance as they occur, and adjusting the foods, activities, and rest that would bring the body and mind back into balance. They will spend part of everyday outside in the fresh air, walking barefoot along the riverbank or pasture, quiet time in solitude to pray and meditate, and doing activities that bring peace, and avoiding activities that bring unnecessary stress.

Breathing is another obvious cycle that gives us information or feedback on what we are experiencing. As the mind calms, the breathing slows. As the mind becomes excitable, the breath quickens its pace. When we are anxious, we tend to breathe shallowly. By changing our breathing, we can actually bring about a change in our emotional state.

You can always depend on your breath to be a reflection of your state of mind. Watch your breath during the day to reconnect with your body and how it is responding. Notice when you are beginning to worry and stop what you are doing; inhale into your belly, long slow breaths, then a longer slow breath exhaling completely. After three or so of these breaths, notice your mind and your mood shifting some.

An excellent book full of great information on respiration is *Breath*, by James Nestor. It covers research on the physiology of breathing, the physical and personal effects of our breathing habits, and how we can improve our lives by improving how we breathe.

You can go within on a regular basis. Create that cycle by acknowledging your spirit daily, with meditation or/and prayer. When you come from meditation back to the outside world, you will bring that inner essence of yourself with you, and it will permeate your day. The more you practice this cycle the more of an effect it will generate. Fulfilling your desires will become easier, as will experiencing peace, contentment, and joy. Meditation will be explained in more detail as we go through the book. It is such an important tool.

Become an active participant in the natural world. Watch the sunrise, go for a walk, and watch the animals going about their day always living in the present moment. Listen to the wind and the water, sit in the grass, jump in a lake, feel and hear the rhythms all about you, because it is *you*, and that connection is vital and healing. Our physiology can then reach coherence with the natural world as well as our inner world, integrating ourselves into both.

Realize how important the sleep cycle is for your wellbeing. Cutting into your night's sleep to catch up on work may help in the immediate future but will be unproductive in the long run.

Financially, *"What are the economic and stock market cycles and how can we take advantage of them?"*

As mentioned previously, many of us are cycling in a limited range of possibilities where matters of income and wealth are concerned. Our income could be topping out at a ceiling but if we figure in inflation, (which has averaged around 3-4% annually for the last 30 years, but has recently been quite a bit higher) we could be losing ground. Many people are cycling through spending sprees until fear painfully grabs them back to the experience of lack. Whenever there is an excess in one direction there is a buildup of force that creates a counter-reaction.

The legend of Lao Tzu is a story of a gifted scholar who lived in China nearly 2600 years ago. He left his words of wisdom at the bequest of the village he was about to leave. There is no way to prove who wrote this magnificent work, but the book, *Tao Te Ching*, is the most translated classic, second only to the Bible. The translation I like is *The Tao of Power* by R.L. Wing. The Tao is the name of the force that operates through the universe, and Wing explains that personal power comes from being in step with the Tao. Since the 1980's physicists have found the book remarkable in its correlation with the new theories of the universe, not to mention behavioral scientists noting that its revelations on the mind are very insightful. Within this book Lao Tzu gives us lessons on how to lead people with the goal of bringing harmony to the world. It states, "The law of polarity changes and evolves all things by acting upon extremes. Extremes are overcharged and begin moving in their opposite direction. Those who follow the Tao avoid extremes and practice moderation and receptivity. *In this way they gain power by moving with the prevailing forces.*" (I think we can relate to this not only in our personal lives but observe this in entities such as organizations and politics.)

Whether we are bouncing back and forth within a range of income, as perhaps a commissioned salesperson might, or spending and hoarding, we are trapped in a dance of excess, allowing polarity to rule us. Try to witness the behavior with the awareness of the observer to get a sense of the impending excess before it is actualized. You will be able to step free when you can recognize what ego needs fuel the behavior. Here, again, we are continuing to ask, "Who am I?". Gently reminding ourselves that we are not the ego, we need not be trapped by the perceived cries of the smaller self. Create a moderate, steady, mindful, and even tempo of earnings; a consistent maintainable output of work, or spending and saving in a level and affordable flow.

There could be physical reasons why one tends to swing between extremes, stemming from a chemical or emotional imbalance, as in bipolar disorder. But they are all linked. We are holistic creatures—it doesn't really work to explain a problem within the context of only one behavior. Sitting down to make out a budget won't completely solve this, but it will help to have an idea of the rhythm that will underlie your success; a rhythm that combines all your behaviors and gives you confidence that you have mastered the cycle. As we care tenderly for ourselves, finding what in our life will improve us spiritually, physically, and emotionally, we will feel more at ease in tackling this type of behavior.

I experienced this trap myself when I was a young stockbroker. After a flurry of activity at work I found myself reaching new highs in my income, only to fall back into inertia, exhausted for a spell. That would break the high-income flow. Any of you on commission may relate to this. I would expend all my energy and emotional currency in a mad frenzied month. After having made great production, I would be spent and barely able to stay on task for the next couple of weeks. This is the cost of extremes. I had to learn 'who I was' and open my eyes to the 'secret' all around me; to ease my income into a steady flow. It was all me! As I learned balance, as I learned to trust myself and mindfully create my intentions, as I learned to connect to my purpose and my higher self, my income became more stable.

Now what about the financial cycles? There are many, but let's look at the economic and market cycles. That is a big enough subject to cover.

Economic

The economy is a vast industry of commerce, the realization of capitalism that beats within our society. The word economy comes from the Greek word *'oikonomos',* which means 'management of the house'. Adam Smith, a Scottish economist and philosopher who lived in the 18th century, wrote *The Wealth of Nations* in 1776. He was very influential to our founding fathers and his ideas can be found in our constitution.

He felt that a free society that is allowed to price goods and services by supply and demand will ultimately create a market with fair prices. And, because of the inherent good of the common people, the government wouldn't have to interfere in this pricing system. By adopting this system there would be the greatest capacity for the spreading of wealth. This is free enterprise. Smith argued that state and personal effort to promote social good are ineffectual compared to unbridled market forces.

Without much interference by the government, what Lao Tzu taught us about extremes is seen, of course, in our economy. When forces go too long in one direction it causes an imbalance, hence a swing in the opposite direction. We see the expansion and recession of the prices of goods and services, trade, corporate growth, and the stock markets. They are always shifting. We have learned to slow these cycles down so that we don't grow too rapidly, which would bring about high inflation, by raising interest rates at pivotal times, which may be seen as manipulative, but we are just affecting the speed of a natural movement. There never has been such a successful system as free enterprise because its very nature is *Natural*. It's like organic farming, using no manmade, artificial means to produce a certain result, relying on nature to do its own thing.

The economy sweeps up and down derived from the mass consciousness of the citizenry. When the masses need a new service or product, it springs in to fill the need by innovation. As consciousness rises in the United States and the world, we will see many changes in the marketplace, but hopefully no changes in the system, because this system acts as we act, behaves as we behave, and changes as we change. Your purpose can be found in the matrix of this system. Whatever you have found to be your dharma (purpose) there is a waiting market for that. The insights you receive that show you a need you can fill are from the same vibrational energies that are creating the specific market that is ready for it.

The Financial Markets and Real Estate

What about the financial markets, specifically the stock and bond markets? They are waxing and waning also. What makes them behave in a cyclical way? What are the cycles in securities markets? Securities are tradable assets and usually when this term is used it refers to stocks and bonds.

In 1792 a group of 24 men in New York City agreed to gather down on a street called Wall Street to exchange their shares of holdings in different companies. In inclement weather they would meet in taverns or kitchens. Finally, in 1821, they moved into a building built for trading in these holdings of business ownership. Since that time the trading of securities has become its own entity, as a component of the economy. It is a gestalt, *a symbolic configuration or pattern of elements so unified as a whole that its properties cannot be derived from a simple summation of its parts.*[2] Since it was first started, this massive trading market has been sliced, diced, analyzed and studied, but no one person has figured out how to out-maneuver the broad markets; that is, consistently bring in returns above and beyond the market as a whole over time. They trade all sizes and types of businesses in a symphony of movements, shifting to the moods and climate of economic news, new innovations, and the trader's

---

2 The American Heritage Dictionary of the English language, 4th edition

optimism or pessimism. But more than just the trader's outlook or the business outlook, it rides on the waves of the country's consciousness. In the short term, it is impossible to predict the movement of an individual stock, let alone the movement of the entire market of stocks. This is backed by several distinguished economists.

For the last 70+ years there has been a wealth of evidence to support the theory that the market is efficient, the current price of a stock is a good determinate of its value at the time, and only new and unknown information will likely change that stock's price significantly. What does that mean? That means if we want to have the power to make money in the stock markets, we can invest and reap the returns from the movements of the broad markets over time. If we plan to find someone whom we hope knows more than we do and pay him or her to find stocks that rise above the broad markets, it turns out to be difficult. Finding a winning stock above all is like trying to guess which fish in a school will jump up out of the wave next. Why not just ride the wave? According to information provided by Morningstar (Morningstar is a company that provides research, rankings, historical movements, and ratings of mutual funds), the great majority of mutual funds do not beat the indexes[3] even half of the time, a very small percentage beat the market over half the time, and this performance is worse than one would expect of random luck!

Let's ride the wave as it rolls forward, with all its fits and starts, lulls and storms, because over the long term it looks like a much better bet. We aren't resisting the cycles; we are flowing with them as naturally

---

3   An index is a representative group of stocks to measure movement of a particular market.

as breathing. In an organic, undisturbed way we can invest in the market naturally, without trying to manipulate it, outdo it, or outperform it. As millions of investors buy, sell, or hold, as the economy expands and recedes, we are quietly capturing the market returns. Within each cycle some asset class is benefiting, so we want to own all the asset classes. For example, we could own the small companies of Europe, the government bonds of Australia, the large companies in Asia, the micro (start-up) companies in the U.S., etc. until we have many, many categories. We can do it in such a way that will reduce our risk.

Of course, real-estate goes through these cycles as well. Both securities and real-estate are usually long-term investments. Some people think they can guess where the market values are in a cycle, but here again, it isn't always easy to know. When you pick any point in time, sometimes you are right on the edge of a turn lower or higher with no signs that you noticed to tell you. Investing for the short term is speculation, and not something most advisors suggest doing. Your abundance isn't something we are going to gamble with!

No one knows the short-term movements in stock market values ahead of time, though you can never run out of opinions of where the 'experts' believe the values are going. Reflect for a moment on the newsworthy events that have impacted our markets in the last 30 years, things that no one, years, months, weeks or even days before, could have guessed. September 11, the bus bombing in London, hurricane Katrina, the Tsunami in Indonesia, the collapse of Enron, the Capitol insurrection, the COVID pandemic, Russia invading Ukraine, and on and on. All of these, and an endless array of lesser events, combined with the prevailing perception of the populace, move our markets in the short term.

We have 24-hour programming giving us every conceivable prognostication regarding stocks, securities markets, industries, economies, the job market, the political climate, commodities, the international trade, real estate markets, currency futures, and on and on. We can look up dozens of websites, each one telling us of the *best* mutual funds to own, what you must do for retirement, how to allocate your 401k, the top 5 stocks you *must* buy, why this mortgage is better, what you should never buy, etc. (I have these phrases on a power point presentation with the soundtrack of drums dramatically beating!) On top of that, there are newsletters you can subscribe to offering special stock recommendations (only if you pay for this information), trading programs that can't lose, workshops to sell you programs that will help you make your fortune, books that teach you the secrets of making money in the stock market, 24 hour e-trade programs on the internet, real estate programs that will tell you it is easy to buy houses with no money, and if you only pay $5,999.00 all these secrets will be yours.

It is an overwhelming task just trying to figure out who to listen to. If we ignore the din from financial advertising and programming, we find, over time, the stock markets and real estate markets continue growing no matter what they've said. By investing for the long term, riding through these market cycles without changing your plan, much of the risk is reduced. Diversifying reduces the risk even further.

Affirmation:

I am a part of this world. As co-creator I pay attention to all the cycles around me and inside me, from the markets to nature, learning to align with them for my greater well-being.

Chapter 4

Point of Power NOW

Where All Our Power Is

"Now is the only time. How we relate to it creates the future. In other words, if we're going to be more cheerful in the future, it's because of our aspiration and exertion to be cheerful in the present. What we do accumulates; the future is the result of what we do right now."
– Pema Chodron

"Eternity is not something that begins after you are dead. It is going on all the time. We are in it now."
– Charlotte Perkins Gilman

It is most apt that this chapter has fallen into the very center of the book without my conscious decision to make it so. When I began writing the book, I outlined seven chapters. They fell in the order they came to me. The first three chapters are about the past, how you got to where you are, and the last three are about where you want to go. And this chapter is about the NOW, the present moment, and what you can glean from this present to better guide you forward. This chapter is about All That Is, which is, always now.

When are we naturally and totally in the present moment? We all haphazardly fall into a deeper awareness of the present quite by accident; for instance, when we see our newborn for the first time, when we gaze upon something of such beauty it lifts us from our everyday concerns, or even during a life changing event; anything that jolts our ego into submission because it is impotent in the face of our powerful spirit. It's at these moments that we experience something that is quite other-worldly, a quiet wonder and stillness. Our judgment is suspended, egoic emotions disappear, and we exist in pure awareness. This is our point of power. All the great religious traditions tell of saints and sages who retreated from the world to seek this awareness through prayer and meditation. Seekers today are still discovering ways to find this deep utter stillness.

We are in the moment when can step outside of ourselves and hold the point of view of the observer. This is important because it is here that we can impove our lives. We can temporarily step away from the ego's emotions, anxieties, and fears. The more we do this the more we realize we are not a victim of any uncomfortable or obsessive thoughts that make our minds race. Again, without these inklings of a higher-self we are caught in a world where our thoughts and beliefs can bring suffering. Being mindful and being aware of the present moment moves us toward the direction of peace and creativity. When the mind is calm, it functions far more effectively! So, in this chapter we will ask:

Spiritually, *How can I connect to the Stillness?*

Physically, *What more is there on current manifestations?*

Financially, *Where is the point of power concerning money?*

Spiritually, *How can I connect to the Stillness?*

How do you attain the skills to create a vibrant, abundant life? What can you do to increase your creativity and be more attuned to your inner guidance? How can you maintain a deep awareness of your physical needs? How can you gain useful insights into your passions and channel that into a purpose? What are the remedies or life hacks that can reduce anxiety, stress, and help regulate the emotional extremes that can throw you off balance? How can you sleep more soundly, improve your memory, laugh more, fulfill desires, gain homeostasis in your physical systems, boost your immune response, let go of bad habits, increase your concentration, and increase your energy? If there were a magic pill that could do all this, people would sacrifice enormously to buy it, don't you think? Yet you already come equipped with the potential to activate this ability within yourself merely by sitting quietly. By not doing anything. By taking a break from your busy life. By turning inward, where the real 'you' resides.

Learning to *meditate* is a gift you can give yourself that can change your life. As I have already said, every religious tradition has its saints, sages and masters that have immersed themselves in prayer and meditation in order to emerge having found enlightenment, wisdom, serenity, and a seemingly complete command of life.

Of course, there is no guarantee of becoming enlightened if you meditate, but you should notice improvements in your life with regular practice. Some people notice changes right away, some after a few weeks, and some only after a few months. If you meditate regularly, you will most likely be richly rewarded. Over the course of my life, I have been aware of many meditation techniques. I have known many people who meditated off and on throughout their lives and I too, have meditated off and on, learning one method, practicing it inconsistently, then dropping it. I repeated this for many years. It wasn't until I stuck with my current method of meditation consistently, over a long time, that I noticed a dramatic, and I do mean dramatic, difference in my life.

I've had several quantum shifts in my lifetime, the kind of changes where I grew and leapt into new arenas of life where I was able to accomplish more. The most significant changes I've experienced (those that made me become conscious of the mastery I have over my life) have occurred since I've been meditating on a regular basis. I was able to realize a long-held dream of mine and left the corporate world. I became self-employed which enabled me to finally embrace my true creativity and talents. I became a business owner, but it didn't stop there. I completely overhauled the way I did business to express my true purpose in life with all the details taking care of themselves! I've learned to trust my gut, my instincts. I began writing in earnest and completed my first novel. My world became filled with a richness of experiences that expanded my definition of happiness. (This is not to say you will forever have no conflicts, no dramatic events in your life. Life always surprises us!)

Your spirit is continually speaking to you in multidimensional ways and by becoming quiet, being in the present, you can connect to it.

In the present, *now*, spirit is speaking to you. It speaks to you through every feeling, visual queue, physical sensation, words you hear, events that pop up, ideas and insights, and people in your life that you admire or identify with, or even those that 'tick you off'. These experiences are all woven in the moment-to-moment creation of your life. When you meditate regularly, you invite your Inner Being to come into your awareness. You will see as if with new eyes. You can also gain more moments in which you will witness your life from your Inner Being's perspective (the observer). Eventually you will hopefully experience your life from higher states of consciousness or higher vibrations.

Regular daily meditation brings out your true essence, *'who you really are'*. As the day wears on, however, this experience wears off. To have the most effect it is recommended you meditate twice a day. Dipping into this stillness is recuperative, and the benefits build on repetition.

Life can be lived with ease. When we have a need, we become aware of a way to fulfill it. As we rise in consciousness it becomes easier to find solutions or better choices. This is a function of the universe and how we, on the spirit level, create our reality. As we move through levels of consciousness, we see the world completely differently at each state. There are states where we experience prosperity in all ways, where we experience no scarcity, where our desires are few, and we know what our true purpose is. Learning to meditate is a stepping-stone toward attaining these states, and it is probably the most dependable method available to us. It's been estimated that it has been used for at least 5,000 years!

We can read lots of books on achieving success, attaining wealth, prestige, power, happiness, wisdom, health, improving relationships, etc. These are great, but why not also utilize this proven technique we call meditation? Conduct your own experiment and try it out for yourself. There are many ways to meditate. Try this once or twice daily for 20 or 30 minutes:

Sit comfortably in a quiet place, eliminate the possibility of interruptions as much as possible, and close your eyes. Relax your muscles, roll your head, neck, and shoulders, and breathe slowly and deeply. Then just begin to watch your breath. Imagine it flowing in and out of your chest. Don't try to control your breathing, just allow it to be. When you notice thoughts or feelings, or even noises, gently let them go from your awareness and go back to watching your breath. Another method is using a word or phrase, called a mantra. A common mantra is So Hum, but you can use any word or phrase like Let go, Let God. Repeat the mantra in your mind, and when you notice you're not thinking the mantra anymore, just gently bring your attention back to it. Be easy with yourself. If you get frustrated because your head keeps filling with thoughts, it is your frustration that will keep you from meditating. The thoughts will always come and go. Just gently let them go each time; it doesn't matter if it is three times or fifty times. You are still getting benefits of the meditation practice. Be easy with yourself, without judgment. When you're done, keep your eyes closed for another few minutes, slowly coming back to your normal thinking.

The physical and mental benefits of meditation are well documented. There are even studies showing that it reverses aging because it reduces the buildup of stress in the physical body that accelerates aging.

Remember, the value of self-discovery is to return ourselves to our true nature and be more aware of who we are; that in and of itself will enhance our wellbeing. By learning what our true nature is we find ourselves unlimited.

The first chapter pointed out what we need to eliminate in our lives to become successful and it is a lifetime process. As you learn more about yourself, you will be better able to reduce what you don't want in your life. The benefit is that the awareness of who you want to be, what you want to do, and what you want to have in your life will naturally increase.

Meditation carries you silently into the now, with purpose and clarity. It is a natural way to raise your consciousness and bring your higher self to the forefront. The material world and all of its concerns fade away into the background, losing the power to distract you. Your ego is stilled into submission like a child in a playful trance.

The ego will fight many attempts to sit quietly, especially here in the West where we are made to feel we are lazy if we are 'not doing anything productive'. Romance the ego—give it tangible rewards to meditate. Approach the time with no thought, like so many habits of your day, like brushing your teeth, driving to work, or checking email. The ego will think of a thousand reasons not to meditate, our thoughts will tell us there are so many things we need to do, but it is doubtful they will raise your consciousness.

Another practice that helps us to be in the present is by 'being' instead of 'doing'. At our very essence we just are. Before we ever did anything at all, we were. We can be aware, as we go about our day, of having the presence of mind to focus on our tasks in a mindful way.

Dr. Jeffrey Brantley, Director of the Mindfulness-Based Stress Reduction Program of the Duke Center for Integrative Medicine, explained what mindfulness is in this way, "We human beings have within us the capacity for deep calm and ease and an awareness that reflects accurately what is happening in the present moment. 'Mindfulness' is a name for this awareness. Mindfulness arises when you pay attention on purpose without judging and in a friendly, allowing way. By paying attention this way and establishing mindfulness of your inner and outer life, moment by moment, a certain ease arises, and you can connect more deeply with what is happening." [1]

The practice of meditation increases the likelihood of successfully mastering mindfulness. When our mind is calm this experience will give itself to you if you have the intention. Practice with small tasks to begin with, ones that don't require you to learn anything new. You can be 'swept up' in the most mundane tasks, like polishing a table, observing the way the grain emerges as the oil spreads across the wood, and the color deepens in richness and depth. One of my favorite mindfulness activities is slicing and chopping vegetables for a meal. It is similar to meditation in that the mind is not on the past or the future. I go about it in a metered, steady way, being careful not to rush. I begin early so I can take my time. This is akin to finding the 'zone' when we are in a creative activity; or when we are on the edge of exceeding our potential in a new skill, yet this is more deliberate...it's mindful. Judgments, emotions, and egoic concerns are quelled. It is like letting God in. We can listen. It is fertile ground for insights because the mind is quieted.

---

1 Quoted in the online magazine, *YogaJournal.com* or *Mindful.org*

Right now, in this moment, all is perfectly as it should be. It is because it is. We are continually distracting ourselves from the perfection of this moment, the full vibrant expression of manifest from unmanifest.

We could be content, enjoying the moment when a tiny thread of a thought presents itself in our mind. A small worry. Then we pull a little tighter on the thread, (paying attention to the worry) and it produces a concern. Our ego starts grasping the thread, pulling more and more, until our peacefulness begins unraveling. Maybe you sat down to write a 'to-do' list or simply began a household chore and you thought of something about work which started a roll of worries. Or you thought of a symptom your spouse or child had, or even yourself, and that started the unraveling. Yet just the moment before all was fine. Your vibration is lowered, and there are powerful techniques to raise it back up before you find yourself spiraling into negative thinking.

Once you discover the train of thinking turning this way, pause. What was it you were getting ready to worry about? Obviously, it is something you don't want. The thought is making you feel bad. It's the *feelings* that sets off the vibrations, and the *thoughts* that led to the feelings, so all you have to do is find a way to derail those thoughts and change those feelings. So many books have been written that give you different ways to do just that. I was raised on *'The Power of Positive Thinking'* by Dr. Norman Vincent Peal, and it gives us a Christian-based process that has influenced millions of people since it was first published in 1956. My vivid vision 'game' probably sprang from his words. Since then, I have come to believe that it is emotions translating into their vibrational counterpart that are the basis for our manifesting. The law of attraction at work.

Here are some methods to 'rebalance' your emotional state or raise your vibrational state.

Shift from what you don't want to realizing what you do want and focus on that.

This works best when you become aware that your thinking is turning negative. You could have just begun to worry about something, or just received news that is upsetting you. As soon as you become aware that your thoughts are making you feel bad, stop, allow yourself to recognize this as something you don't want, and mentally search for the version of that topic that you do want. I've used this successfully. For instance, I ran various ads for my financial business in different publications. I'd developed a new ad campaign, letting the publications know what I wanted to run, how I wanted it to look and what I wanted it to say. One publication sent me a proof of the new ad which wasn't acceptable, wording or image-wise. I had had problems in the past with this particular publication, so my faith in them was already compromised. The advertising executive told me he would go back to the drawing board and email me a new proof so I could see it before it ran. I got busy and forgot about it. The day before it was to run, I remembered with a start that I never got a new proof! I phoned the ad executive trying to remain calm and optimistic! (You cannot cover up irritation with false happiness!) I was told, oops sorry, it is running and he would send me a copy of what ran! Well, my emotions went from irritation to anger when I saw it. It was awful; there was even a misspelled word in the large lettering, making it impossible to miss. I shot an e-mail to the publication of its unacceptability and went on to other things. But when I got home, I knew that subject would be ruminating in the back of my mind, making me feel bad if I didn't change my thinking on it. So, I sat down and asked myself what this was telling me. I learned what it was I didn't want; depending on others that don't understand what image I wanted to portray, having ads run that I hadn't approved, and having ads run with mistakes in them!

Now, since I want to feel good about my advertising, in fact I want to feel good about all aspects of my business, all I had to do is focus on what I did want. I wanted to have people to work with on my marketing that were trustworthy, dependable, and really understood the mission of my business; people who would take the concepts that are at the heart of what I do and create marketing material that would convey that. That's all! I immediately began feeling better. As my vibration rose ideas began coming to me. The thread turned to a string of good thoughts. And in a matter of a few minutes the owner of a design and marketing firm popped into my mind. A few months before this fiasco, she had offered to design and schedule all my marketing for a small fee. She had worked with me closely on a couple of my projects and designed beautiful images for my business. I relaxed into the joy of knowing my future promotions were safe in her hands. I couldn't wait until the next morning to tell her! I slept soundly.

You have the power to change your reality on a dime. It rests in the now. Truth lies in our laps waiting for our recognition of it. And the truth is that you create your own reality.

But what happens when you have strong feelings, and feel bad? Everyone does. What do you do? What can you do? Everyone has different ways to cope or self-sooth, perhaps some you even learned from your family. There are so many. A few are: take a walk, read something inspiring, sit by a window and gaze outside, take a nap, do something creative, work out, yard work, fix something, call a friend, or lay on the grass and look up at the stars or clouds.

Another practice is to develop a habit of shifting your awareness from the ego to your higher-self, the observer. As those peace destroying thoughts appear, stay connected to the knowingness of your spirit. Relax your body, don't resist the tightness, that only increases it. Let it go and feel the tension leave. Whatever worry that started it was probably from an old, repressed hurt within you. Doing this over and over can remove it.

In Indian philosophy, past traumas and bad experiences are called samskaras, and they are held within the body on an energetic level if they aren't processes and released. It's important to mention this here because we don't advise to simply repress bad feelings. It is good practice to notice when a bad feeling comes up, where in the body it is felt, and allow yourself to be present with it until it dissipates.

Allow emotions to flow through you with acceptance. Stand back and notice them. Attempting to hold them back, denying them, pushing against them, fencing them in, encourages them to exist behind the fence like junkyard dogs barking as you move by them, standing ever ready to beg your attention again and again. Accept them and they turn into lap dogs.

I'm adding a note here, because sometimes in life we get thrown a devastating blow and I don't mean to minimize this. When I received the news that one of my adult children had a profound diagnosis, there wasn't a simple cure for my pain. It took months for me to climb out of the deep hole it sent me into, and I utilized all the methods I knew, especially meditation, to help me cope and regain my balance. I thank God I had these practices.

Physically, *What more is there on current manifestations?*

What we perceive about people and things around us and what we believe about it is our current manifestation.The act of observing our environment and the people in it creates the canvas to make it into what we want to live, see, and experience now.

How again, do your thoughts affect your outer world? On one level it is simply your memories, attention and thoughts that lay a foundation for a belief; and beliefs are the constructors of our lives. For example, if you know someone that did something cruel and you have seen or heard evidence, you may decide that that person is a 'bad' person. Whenever you think about that person you add more negative thoughts to their image in your mind. Soon you see no good in the person because you believe it isn't there, even though intellectually you know this isn't so. Belief and intellect are often at odds with one another.

Everyone has known or been in a family that has this experience: let's say family dynamics in one particular family are functioning in such a way that the psychological buildup of 'steam' (inner negative energies) is expressed through their daughter. This daughter has out-of-control tantrums, is manipulative, and displays inconsolable crying—during which the parents and siblings look on, wide-eyed, without seeing a cause!

125

The parents may begin to think this child is the 'bad' child. These thoughts build upon themselves at every incident until the parents have created a belief about this child that is very narrow, eclipsing the gestalt of a total human being full of a huge variation of attributes, until the only thing they see is a problem child. Now the child only receives attention when she conforms to their belief. They no longer see her when she is being kind, or sharing, or gentle. That doesn't register for them. How do you think she responds to this? Yep, she eventually conforms to what they expect, slowly realizing that her good behavior is ignored, getting no attention, so she increases the 'bad' behavior because every child craves attention!

The world functions in this way. When you believe, because of a succession of thoughts, that you aren't smart enough, good enough, or lucky enough to be financially successful, you miss all the cues around you saying anything different. You aren't aware of the opportunities parading by you, right now. How many people have you known that complain about how much things cost, what a bad deal they got, that they can never get ahead, and they obviously do not feel abundant? What we pick up on in the material world always goes along with our feelings and reactions. Our feelings attract more of the same in our perception, so we continue to notice what we don't want.

Since you (from your ego's standpoint) are a compilation of all the thoughts and feelings that you have had in the past, you now have an opportunity to turn the tide if you so desire. Instead of reacting to your life's events, create them! Often times it isn't necessary to unearth the whys of a belief, it is easier to build new habits of thinking.

When we first become aware of how powerful our own thinking is, it can create a sense of anxiety worrying about what is going on in our heads all day. But give yourself the space to make mistakes and fall back on old habits, because as long as you hold the intention, you will make progress. Remember, time is fluid and entirely an ego perception, so you have all the time you need. Remember to stop and relax.

When we learn a new skill or want to put a new spiritual method to work in our life, we get so excited, and so impatient, that the combination sometimes causes a knot in our stomach! Stop, breathe into the tightness, and tell yourself it will all unfold for you: it doesn't have to happen in this moment.

Your life experience will follow your intentions and desires as you grow in the knowledge of how to change your thinking and beliefs. It is your job to set your intentions, and notice the conditions, ideas and opportunities that are before you that will enable your goals to come about.

Here is the secret: start with intentions that hold no resistance within you. Begin with something that you can believe. If you can't picture yourself in your dream job just yet, can you picture yourself enjoying your current job more? If you can't visualize yourself having one million dollars in the bank without resistance in your gut, can you visualize a thousand? If we believe it isn't possible, we won't shoot for it. So, begin there. When you imagine your desire fulfilled, without resistance, it feels good. And the good feeling will enhance your intentions, bringing your vibration in line with your desire.

Finally, there is another method that I have found invaluable to challenge those thoughts that cause negative emotions. A great tool for this was created by Byron Katie and it's called *The Work*. It consists of a simple worksheet to follow until the suffering thoughts are brought to a standstill. I have her app on my phone. Just google it.

Where is the point of power concerning money?

Since money is an expression of freedom, it also only exists in the present moment, to be called forth by our underlying desires and needs and the vibrations they emit. This moment is pregnant with all of your financial yearnings, yet your vibrations could be obstructing the avenue to their realization.

I had a client who was 'desperately', 'frustratingly' trying to discover what her block was to financial ease, and I told her about another client. The second client, I will call Grace, was around 70; she inherited some money about 15 years before, not a huge amount, but a good sum. She spends on whims and really has no overall plan. I just observe her in amazement. She has never seemed to worry about money; on the contrary, she is oblivious! Grace flows in sheepishly requesting a withdrawal for what she excitedly describes as a wonderful, lovely object to purchase. She doesn't seem to worry about tomorrow, she has a wonderful faith, and she dotes on all her family members. Money is a pleasurable activity to her, something she views with gratitude and grace. She doesn't have exorbitant desires, but they aren't small either. I explained this to the first client; not to suggest she try to be like Grace, but to show her there are other paradigms surrounding money that don't include angst. She called three weeks later to tell me she was 'invoking' the persona of my 70-year-old free-spirited client. Grace had become an archetype for her. That is one way we can learn to eradicate our blocks, and a very creative way indeed!

Archetypes are powerful energies in the collective consciousness. Dr. Carl Jung understood the forceful dynamics inherent in archetypes and the ways in which people of different cultures use them to create, heal and manifest what they desire. These archetypes exist in the Collective Mind ready to be channeled by us all. You can find a persona, living, dead or mythical, and invoke those attributes that you admire — those that you want to express. These attributes are already inside of you. Some are dominant, others are latent. Those that you are wishing to have can gain in energy and be brought forth. We certainly see this in children. They channel their heroes and heroines with glee!

Which Archetype represents prosperity to you? Who lives in a manner that speaks of unlimited spending enjoyment? Picture yourself looking out of the eyes of a person who lives this way. Pretend, even if it feels funny. It will grow on you.

Using Gratitude, Tithing

It is such a blessing to yourself when you pause and appreciate what you have now. There are some concrete things you can do to anchor yourself in deep appreciation. Appreciation opens you up to attract even more of what you are currently grateful for. It is with gratitude that I pay my monthly bills.

Every time you sign a check you can mentally say, 'thank you'. How wonderful that the universe is fulfilling your obligations.

As you write your checks or click that pay button, instead of feeling a tightness in your gut or even fear because you worry about depleting your funds, feel the gratefulness that you can pay the person or company that you owe, and in doing so continue the circle of energy that fulfills us all. As it goes out, so it will return. You can even put thank you in the memo field, I bet someone will appreciate that!

Send out thank you cards. How about sending one thank you card in the mail per week? If someone in your employ does something exemplary, or is just a conscientious worker, reinforce that, but make sure they know what it is specifically that they do that is appreciated. Giving broad compliments is great, like, "you are such a hard worker" but it's even better to comment and recognize those details where someone took special care, "I noticed you did more than I asked, you even cleaned out that old storage closet!"

Of course, it doesn't stop at employees, maybe a family member did something special for you, a friend that listened, a business relationship like your insurance agent or advisor who helped you out, or someone who gave you good counsel. I know as an advisor when I get a thank you note of appreciation, I don't forget that. I can feel my vibration rise, and it could come on a day that it is just what I needed!

In your Now, look at what you are grateful for and how you can show appreciation.

Pay Yourself First-PYF

Before you write those checks and tithe, pay yourself. You are your first obligation. Without you all the rest wouldn't matter. It's a way of blessing yourself, recognizing your importance, your divine place in the universe. PYF was mentioned in Chapter Two on setting up an emergency fund. Whether it is $5 or $500 isn't the point right now; developing the habit of paying yourself first will do two things. 1) Watching the money build will give you good feelings of safety, confidence, hope, even excitement and 2) It is a way to honor yourself, realize your immeasurable worth.

If you already have an emergency fund in a bank account or money market, invest the rest. Let's look again at investing in today's market.

Today's Values, Markets and Services

In the perfection of the moment all prices of goods and services are accurate. The values of properties, stocks, bonds, products, jobs, consumables, futures, options, and services are fully where they should be at any given time. This, as said in an earlier chapter, was the proposal of the Scottish philosopher and economist, Adam Smith, as well as the sages throughout history who stated there is perfection in the moment; all is as it should be. Once we accept the state of things exactly as they are, we create space. New and currently unknown information and experience will move values and events in our future. But by not accepting the current condition, fighting against it and resisting, just makes us unhappy.

The 7 Habits of Successful Investors

I wrote this based on my observations and knowledge gained over the last 30+ years in the financial business. I noticed that the people who are successful investors all have something in common. They all may have different methods of saving and investing, but they had one main commonality, peace of mind. They're confident, have faith in their program, and have the following 7 attributes described below.

Habit No. 1 Ability to Delay Gratification

This reminds me of a study I learned about in a college psychology class. Researchers took a group of 4-year-olds and one by one called them into a room. The room contained only a table and a chair. The four-year-old was told to have a seat. The researcher placed a marshmallow on the table in front of the child and told the child that he had to leave for a few minutes, and that if she waited until the researcher returned before eating the marshmallow, he would give her 3 more! Well, you can imagine how hard this would be for a small child, yet some were able to restrain themselves for many minutes before the researcher came back to give them the reward of more. The study followed these children through school and found the children who were able to delay gratification, who could deny themselves the current reward for a better payoff down the line, ended up being more successful than the others. The impulsive ones more often had a harder time planning for future rewards, rather, grabbing for today and having less for tomorrow. This indulgent behavior allows the ego to dictate decisions. Delayed gratification is a simple concept having a profound impact on our lives and can mean the difference between a successful investor and one who is continually disappointed. Why is that?

A successful investor has the discipline to hold on to a well-diversified portfolio when times are dark, (while others bail out—eat their marshmallows now for fear there will be no more), knowing time will ultimately bring them the better returns, not some 'hot' stock or get rich quick scheme. That is why coaching has evolved. Many advisors have been using coaching without knowing it; they naturally inspire, motivate, and encourage clients in challenging situations. A trained financial coach can help those of you who missed the mark by not waiting, and help you achieve your plan with mega-doses of patience, reassurance, information, and inspiration!

Habit No. 2 Investing for Life

Investing isn't a race with a finishing line. There is no magic date in the future that you must stop investing and go to cash, or even all bonds. This, however, is a very common misconception. I know, because so many people have told me when they are going to retire and that they will invest for retirement 'until then'. "And then what?" I ask them. Some people just haven't thought beyond the big retirement date. They may have a vague idea to move out of the market to protect their money after they retire, but cash is a poor producer of income. You could go to the bank with your savings from your investments, but you may run into trouble eventually because bank savings accounts and CDs run the risk of trailing behind inflation. This means your money loses 'buying value' as time marches on, and it can eventually affect your standard of living.

Successful investors know that to stay ahead they need to always keep their money invested. Historically, the broad stock markets have earned a higher rate of return than the rate of inflation, which is what makes them so attractive to successful investors. The S & P 500 Index has historically averaged higher than the rate of inflation. A well-diversified portfolio can produce income for retirees and can potentially produce it far longer than a bank account could *if* it has appropriate risk management built into it. Successful investors know time will smooth out the dramatic ups and downs caused by events. They know staying invested year after year will increase the likelihood of a better return. That is why you see people fully invested in their 50's, 60's, 70's, 80's and beyond. Some might say, "But I am 75 years old, I can't take that kind of risk." Certainly, the portfolio can be adjusted for a person's age and risk tolerance. It would be unacceptable to put a risk-adverse

75-year-old in a portfolio of 100% stocks. But he may feel comfortable in a portfolio that is 75% short term corporate and government bonds and 25% in highly diversified stocks with the objective of providing enough growth to keep up with inflation.

The very wealthy already know this. They have managers and coaches who make sure their money is invested wisely. Corporations know this, pension plan administrators know this, and even non-profit organizations know this. They know it would be imprudent not to invest idle money. Investing is for life. Let your kids cash it out if you've not spent it all! (They would be better off if they continued investing and monitoring the portfolio, though!)

Habit No. 3 Ignoring the Hype

This is hard to do if you are susceptible at all to today's crazy media-soaked world, but a successful investor doesn't wait for direction from a TV show, or a friend or the neighbor down the street. She doesn't compare her portfolio to her friends' and families' portfolios. She has a plan of her own. She knows what she is doing and why. No one on a cable financial show cares as much about her own future as she does. They care about ratings, so they can get more advertising dollars.

Dr. David Walsh of the *National Institute on Media and the Family* gives parents a fascinating overview of the history of television. He shows how easy it was to sell advertising in the 1950's. There were only 3 TV channels and everybody watched those three. The wholesome family fare was interesting to the audience, it was new and delicious and exciting. I remember our first television when I was four, and we were so excited to watch when the shows aired.

As time went on the networks became more competitive with each other, more comedies and more dramas were added to their lineups. As the television landscape grew, they were soon competing for big advertising dollars, so they added even more riotous comedy, along with more action, more adventure, with more sophisticated and exciting entertainment like cowboy shows complete with horse chases and gun fights.

Time passed and the need for bigger audience numbers started to dominate their business strategies. The networks had to continue adding new cutting-edge shows to keep the viewers glued to their network, so they added sexual innuendo, more violence, comedy with sexual topics, etc. How does all of this relate to investing? The financial cable news networks are no exception. These networks' sole purpose is to amass advertising dollars. Period. It is not to make you rich. In their frantic competition they bellow out with urgency the best mutual funds you MUST own, the hottest stocks of the year, the show you MUST listen to if you are going to retire successfully, the strategy you MUST use to retire early, where the market is going, what is going up, what is going down, and on and on.

Jane Bryant Quinn, a past columnist with the Washington Post, described this type of information as 'investment pornography' (the depiction of investment and/or financial information in a sensational manner to titillate or arouse a quick, intense, emotional reaction).[2] There is no way an investor can follow all of these recommendations, or pay complete attention, even if it were advantageous to do so. Add to this swirling mass, additional information from the internet, publications, friends, family, coworkers and neighbors' opinions, and

---

2 Source: Investorhome.com

you have a hurricane of noise. Add to that noise current events that constantly bombard us, filling up our airwaves with 'breaking news' that hits every channel every five minutes. I can remember a time when the term 'breaking news' was something rare, used only for unusual and notable events!

Our successful investors are not deterred by all of this noise, or even national or global calamities. When we step back to look at history, we see what the stock market did after the dire past events in our country's past; Japan's attack on Pearl Harbor, the Cuban missile crisis, President Kennedy's assassination, the invasion of Kuwait, September 11th, the housing crisis in 2008, the COVID pandemic and beyond, etc. We can look at one month, six months, and one year later. In most cases any losses were recouped after one year![3] Successful investors have learned to stay the course when others get frightened and grab their marshmallows and run.

Successful investors don't worry about others' opinions, and they don't worry someone is getting a better return than they are; someone probably is. Successful investors know they have a plan, why their plan works, and how it works! They don't need to hear the latest fad, the latest 'hot stock,' option play, or oil forecast; they simply dance to their own drummer, knowing these are just new ideas for packaging the same good ole' stocks and bonds. Some of these new ideas could have layers of costs.

Successful investors have learned to tune out all this noise, realizing it has nothing to do with them and their own plans for their money. A successful investor can rely on his investment coach to help him adhere to his goals.

---

3 Report: ' Dramatic events in History', data courtesy of Dow Jones Indexes.

Habit No. 4: Understanding the Risk

We can reduce but never completely eliminate risk. We face risk every day; when we take a shower, drive to work, and cross the street, etc. If we leave our money safely tucked into a bank account, we are exposed to inflation risk, where the value of a dollar could be eroding faster than the interest earned. Inflation is why everything continues to cost more as the years go by, and to eliminate this risk, our money must grow faster than or equal to the inflation rate.

There is another risk called capital risk. If we pick a stock or mutual fund to invest in, there is a risk it could decline quite dramatically. What does the successful investor do? Successful investors assess the risk when developing their investment portfolios. The economist Harry Markowitz devised a Noble Prize-winning method of measuring the risk in a portfolio. A particular portfolio mix of certain categories of stocks and bonds can be measured for the range it will likely move up and down in value. Without getting too complex, suffice it to say that the lower the standard deviation (the risk ratio) is, the narrower the volatility range. If a portfolio has a very low standard deviation, like five, the portfolio isn't going to move markedly up or down, but neither are the returns going to be very high.

Small company foreign stocks have had a history of a standard deviation over 30, which gives you an idea of how that market could move up and down (big swings). A successful investor knows what the probabilities are for his portfolio and uses this information to decide how to build it. A successful investor knows about how much a portfolio will go down before he loses sleep! This is his risk tolerance—and this information must be balanced against the potential rewards for a certain mix of investments.

Some risks are prudent and some are imprudent. If you wanted to get somewhere quickly and you were running late, would driving down the street at 100 miles an hour be a prudent risk? Does the risk outweigh the reward? Maybe, if someone's life depended on it and you were driving them to the hospital. But if you were just going to the grocery store, that is not a prudent risk. The reward of getting to the grocery store a few minutes earlier doesn't outweigh the risk you just took. A successful investor wouldn't put all his money into one penny stock, for example. That would be an imprudent risk. Its undiversified, its gambling, and the risk outweighs the potential for a high return. Yet many, many unsuccessful investors do just that, hoping 'this time' they will hit the jackpot.

Successful investors, on the other hand, stick to the old fashioned tried-and-true method of building an investment portfolio with the amount of risk they know they can handle in exchange for the potential return, and then quietly go about their lives, letting the markets do the work for them.

Habit No. 5: Diversifying

Lack of diversification increases potential risk. Spreading your investment among different asset classes will lessen risk because it lowers the standard deviation ratio. Successful investors find out what the risk level and potential return is for different mixes of asset classes and then take action. Looking at an actively traded mutual fund manager's 'track record' on past performance including past standard deviation does not tell the savvy investor what the future volatility, or standard deviation of that mutual fund will be next year. Why? Because we are talking about a mutual fund that is actively traded, the manager buys and sells securities throughout the year, changing the mix. Sometimes the changes are minor, but often the changes can modify the volatility quite significantly.

In the late nineties, during the technology stock boom, the technology stocks were bringing in such massive returns that even managers who usually held stuffy old conservative companies in their portfolios couldn't resist gobbling up torrents of tech stocks. When in 1999, the tech bubble burst, we found out too late that a great number of funds held too many tech stocks, making them vulnerable and volatile. It didn't help to know what the volatility rating in a fund was the year or two before; it didn't apply in the year 1999!

What successful investors know is the way in which the broader markets and asset classes have behaved in the past. We have several decades of research by such notables as Mr. Harry Markowitz, Eugene Fama, Kenneth French, Roger Ibbotson, and many more. These accomplished economists have quietly studied the volatility behavior of all the different markets of the world and what happens to that volatility in a portfolio mix as different asset classes are added or taken away.

If our investor has a portfolio of nothing but short-term government bonds, that will have low volatility, or not much risk, not much drop or increase in value, but what if he added 50% of the Standard & Poor's 500 stocks? He's probably doubled his risk, and potentially doubled his return. But then he might add some corporate bonds, lowering the risk but still keeping some of the higher return. Then he might try adding big blue chip foreign stocks. Now he's increased the return.

As he adds to his portfolio, he weighs the risk versus the reward at every step, until he comes upon a mix that has historically had the long-term return he desires for the volatility, or standard deviation that he can live with. This may look like using past performance to choose portfolios, but there actually is a huge difference. Past performance is the term used to describe an active fund manager's record of managing a portfolio of securities. The active mutual fund manager is buying and selling stocks or bonds; deciding what to keep, when to dump and what to go out and buy in the broader markets. The mutual fund at any given time could hold 150 stocks chosen from an asset class that may have 1500, or even 2000 stocks. The manager is counting on his or her picks to do better than the total return of the entire asset class.

Making good choices isn't so easy, and most managers don't.[4] It can be very costly as well. We believe the broader market return is quite healthy and generous left on its own. It is like an organic way to invest. By buying the broad markets, you receive the broad market returns. It is simpler because there is no stock picking. This is similar to buying an index fund.[5]

That can save money on costs as well. Our investor's strategy then becomes a dance of adding and subtracting different asset classes. There are a few good mutual fund companies to choose from that do this very thing, and one can buy the asset classes and hold them. That is very diversified. And fortunately, there are money managers who use this very investing philosophy. It is called structured or passive investing.

---

4 Large U.S. blend funds active fund manager's performance compared against the unmanaged S & P 500 Index from 1995 to 2004. This showed 10% of the managers seemed to do better, or beat the market at least half of the time. However 90% of the mutual funds managers consistently seemed to do worse than the S&P 500. This is less than one would expect of random luck! Source: Morningstar

5 A large representation of an asset class, such as the S & P 500, and these can also be purchased.

Habit No. 6: Rebalancing (Buy Low, Sell High)

Our successful investor has now built a portfolio that matches his temperament, goals, risk-tolerance and time horizon. Does he just sit back and wait? He could. But within a few short years, his allocation will shift. Some components of the portfolio will go down and some will go up (this we know), and when this happens, pretty soon his percentages are different than when he started. Let's say he began his portfolio with 75% stocks and 25% bonds. Then the stocks dropped over the next two years, and bonds rose in value, until his new mix is: stocks 60% and bonds 40%. This could change the outlook for his portfolio. It isn't as exposed to stocks as it was, but when the stock market goes up over time, he won't see as much gain as before. Time will gradually change any portfolio mix, creating a new expected return for the new composition.

Successful investors already know this, so they prepare ahead of time, and make rebalancing the portfolio an important part of their plan. This means on a regular basis (normally either quarterly or annually), their portfolio is analyzed by their manager to see if the allocations of their desired mix have changed too much. In the case of the 75% stock and 25% bond portfolio, when it shifted to the 65% stock and 35% bond allocation, the manager would sell 10% of the bond portfolio (sell high), and add that money to the stock portfolio (buy low!) The result? —He will be taking a profit from what has gone up and buying what has become cheaper. Past research has shown that just by rebalancing regularly investors can add more growth per year!

Habit No. 7: Attitude and Beliefs

After all those suggestions, you may think this is an afterthought. Without the proper attitude, however, the other suggestions are just a bunch of words; without the proper beliefs, the other habits will not ensure your success.

What do investors with an attitude for success look like to us?

They are confident that the markets work, believe in supply and demand—that the pricings in the market are an accurate measure of the market's worth, and their attitude is—let the markets work for us! They believe in the principles first set forth by Adam Smith, which is allowing society to set prices for goods and services by supply and demand which in turn will provide the opportunity for the largest segment of a population to become prosperous. Thus, our successful investor believes the pricing system in the markets work, that only unknown information will change the prices, and that no one can consistently and reliably forecast the way the market moves.

He believes that while the movements of the markets will create challenges for him because of his emotional and instinctive reactions, his knowledge, together with his financial advisor, will help him stay true to his plan. He isn't afraid to open his statements but does so with curiosity and understanding. If he has questions or concerns, he jots them down for the next meeting or teleconference with his financial advisor/coach.

He doesn't expect to make frequent changes to his portfolio because of what is going on in the markets; the time to change the portfolio is when his situation changes. He has seen the research on how the stock markets react to dramatic events in history and the subsequent recovery over time, so he keeps this in mind when the climate is producing fear in the public psyche, with alarming 'breaking news' daily. His portfolio is properly diversified to manage the risk of these events. He expects the portfolio to decline at such times. He expects to achieve the long-term returns commensurate with the markets. His attitude is that the market returns are generous, and beating the market rarely can be done in a consistent, low-cost, low-risk manner.

My message is simple:

- Invest in equities
- Diversify in different asset classes
- Develop a long-term plan
- Rebalance

Affirmation:

I pause throughout the day, taking note of the present moment; in its richness, filled with the life force that connects me right now to All That Is. I receive all the divine support I need for my abundant, thriving life.

Chapter 5

House

Our 'house' is consciousness—consciousness
in all its forms.

It is where we all live.

*"Keeping your body healthy is an expression of gratitude to the
whole cosmos-the trees, the clouds, everything."*
– Thich Nhat Hanh

A house can mean many different things. It can mean a structure, and when filled with a family it turns into a home. It is where living takes place. It is our foundation. Since we all derive from, and exist within consciousness, consciousness is our house too.

What is consciousness anyway? If you take the broadest view, everything is consciousness. And there really is no other view. To reiterate, quantum physics researchers are coming up with models of the universe that support the idea that there is a matrix underlying everything, and it responds to every action and thought. We know that when we reduce matter to its smallest particle we eventually arrive at pure energy. I covered this briefly in chapter one. Could this matrix, from which all arises, be what we call God? That is where this research seems to be leading.

For every stage in human thought and behavior on the evolutionary scale, there is an observable level of consciousness from our very primal, survival-driven beginnings, to more and more awareness. This is the leading edge of hard science today. What still bewilders scientists however, is that it seems nearly impossible to transcend this current edge of research to understand the physical universe more fully. Achieving that level of insight will be an enormous paradigm shift.

We cannot unlock the knowledge to be found in the higher levels of consciousness by using the normal operating mode of our ego and merely observing or manipulating matter. Intellect can only take us so far. We must go beyond the ego; tapping into the greater matrix of consciousness wherein knowledge is something of which one has direct inner-perceptual experience.

Down through the ages there have been many who offered a mysterious, magical, and intriguing view of the world. Most of these teachers told their students that they, too, could transcend egoic suffering and be free. They left a map of sorts for us to follow. With the aid of past and current enlightened teachers, we too can learn to traverse these levels and reach those places inside us that hold the infinite knowledge that is our birthright.

There is a whole spectrum of consciousness levels at work on our planet today. There are extremes in almost all topics, ideas, and actions. One thing we have going for us is the extraordinary number of humans on the earth today that are raising their awareness. This has never happened before. These 'awakened' individuals are rising out of a world of contrast seeking to find which way to go, where to focus, how to help.

You will notice the best teachers today are all saying the same thing. Evolve. Grow, be aware, go within, be peaceful, find yourself, and realize who you really are. That's all. And when we do that—we will be aligned with the greater reality and what we do will be for the higher good of all.

Our house, too, can be our financial house. What is its structure and strength? Just as it helps in your financial life to have a plan, goals, a vision of your success, so too does it help to see where you are going on your path to raise your consciousness and find your own purpose. A scale of the levels of consciousness makes it easier to see where you are. Then you can see the next step on your path to financial health and what it will take to define and realize your financial goals. This will be linked back to money consciousness, too.

In the works of Dr. Don Edward Beck, Ph. D. with his *Spiral Dynamics*, Dr. David Hawkins, M.D. Ph. D. with his *Map of the Scale of Consciousness*, Ken Wilbur, philosopher with his *Integral Psychology* that combines consciousness study with spirit, psychology and therapy, and many others, we have ample resources to devise a map for ourselves to see a clear path for financial success.

And we mustn't leave out the ancient Vedic seers, who somewhere around 5,000 years ago left us their map through the *Rig Veda, Bhagavad Gita,* along with other amazing other-worldly bodies of work.

Power comes directly from our source of consciousness, and this kind of power gives us far more control over our lives than physical force. There is also a graduating shift in awareness of one's own destiny. Take the example of people in South Carolina when questioned about what they planned to do and how they felt when they heard the news of a hurricane heading for their shores and orders to evacuate. The most aware/conscious group made concrete plans because they were internally directed to take action to minimize losses. This group felt it was up to them to take responsibility for what happens in their personal experience.

The reaction in the least aware groups was more passive, they felt that whatever happened to them was fate. They felt vulnerable and powerless to change what they saw as inevitable and remained unmoved to take action that could lead to a better outcome. With little sense of their own agency to change their situation, they placed that responsibility outside of themselves. Powerlessness.

In any kind of event, there is a wide range of preparedness and responsibility that is determined by where someone's consciousness falls on the scale or map. (Socio-economic status doesn't always dictate what level of consciousness a person operates on, but it is often a factor.)

The Map of Money Consciousness™ is influenced by the works of the above-mentioned authors and is distilled down to a simplistic map that we can readily use. The Map of Money Consciousness™ is an ongoing, flexible map because new ideas are always emerging from the leading edge of consciousness studies. Dr. Don Beck is right when he explains how our growth is in a spiral, and Ken Wilbur adds that the levels we move through remain present within our current level. We are an accumulation of our personal history and that of the whole human species. The Vedic word for this is Karma.

This is a deep, endless subject of research, and by no means am I able to explain it in a concise form. My intention is to give a glimpse into these amazing ideas so that when you view the levels of consciousness you have some reference.

Consciousness, in all its forms is the physical universe, an intelligent universe, our material world, including our physical bodies, and financial assets. Nothing is outside of consciousness. Out of awareness come thought, energy, and lastly physical manifestation.

Keep this in mind when reading the three sections of this chapter:

> **Spiritually**, *Consciousness and the Field*
>
> **Physically**, *Our Home, Body, and Earth, Abundantly Alive*
>
> **Financially**, *Our Financial House*

> **Spiritually**, *Consciousness and the Field*

We live in a fluid, ever-changing universe that includes our mind, and emotions.

We are the universe aware of itself, all that we can see, sense, and experience within and without. To put it another way, the universe/ God is experiencing humanity through us, through our perceptions.

We know the physical universe is expanding. We can measure this. But we are also always expanding as consciousness. In all ways. With every experience we learn. We grow. Whether suffering or elated, consciousness benefits, consciousness expands. Of course, some may like to use the word God for consciousness and certainly that fits.

Out of God, consciousness, everything is manifested in endless ways. Out of this grand mystery, we exist. We draw from infinite energy to form our world, our experiences, and events. From our emotional and intellectual climate, ideas, thoughts, and plans arise!

Therefore, building the best 'climate' within us is essential in creating the life we want. We have the power. When we use force, push through obstacles, extend ourselves exhaustively, we use our own limited power.

How do we use this 'power' then? By using the cycles from Chapter Three. Connecting to the natural flow of existence, neither hurried nor stagnated. Here are a few examples:

- Be filled with passion before you act
- Make decisions taking your gut responses into account
- Drop your attention from head to heart
- Have a regular meditation practice
- Keep a regular schedule
- Read inspiring works
- Listen to your intuition
- Regularly write down your goals

Using your power means taking action, making decisions, and moving forward when you are aligned with your inner being. This happens when you are feeling inspired, filled with appreciation, love, joy, or confidence. Usually, it is accompanied with a peaceful feeling. A calm excitement, (oxymoron!). For instance, if there is more fear than excitement, it may be a good idea to wait until that fear diminishes. This doesn't mean you shouldn't go forward, just perhaps wait a little while.

Patience. Look back on your life and notice when there were times where you jumped too soon. Made a quick decision that didn't work out well. There is no rush, there is no reason to hurry, you have the time you need.

Using power, you have clarity. By closely flowing into pure consciousness, you loosen the drags of the material world. This is your true home. Our House where we all live.

Prosperity Consciousness

During times of economic uncertainty, the ego can rush to distrust, fear the future, buy into the hype and become overtaken with distress. Many people make decisions that thwart their chances of becoming financially successful.

First of all, we are innocent beings with no outward means of recognizing what is true and what is untrue on the surface of life. So, if you are feeling unprosperous, it isn't your fault! The ego and the mind readily pick up on negative ideas from the vast, pervasive media effusing imminent disasters!

Our peace and prosperity lie in the stillness beneath the noise. Our inner being has no reason not to trust life completely, and that includes our financial prosperity. So, how do those who are financially prosperous look to us? What do they do, think, and believe? They all come from different backgrounds and different belief systems, but they have a few things in common:

1) They expect to be comfortable financially

Whether they grew up in a family that had prosperity expressed or grew up in extreme poverty, they saw themselves becoming prosperous with no resistance to it. It wasn't a goal to be reached someday (putting it in the future holds it away) but an essence felt inside of financial ease.

2) This ease is not disturbed by temporary events.

We are always going through a variety of events seen as good or bad. In the last 40 years the bad news has been chased down by the media to an extreme level, portraying our future as dismal, thus generating fear. I've watched my successful clients during these times, and they remain calm hearing these reports, especially if they know what they are doing and why. They have a confidence that comes from their Inner Being instead of looking outside of themselves for validation of their choices.

3) They have a long-term outlook.

They have a long-term view of the markets too and know they will experience down periods. They don't magnify current events, but rather examine history and look at how they have survived so many different kinds of storms, financial as well as in other areas of life. Connecting facts and research lends the ego a perspective that can't be argued away. Everything is constantly changing. So, if it seems very bad now, that will certainly change.

4) They believe in the inherent goodness of life.

Many probably don't even realize they do this, but I can clearly see that they have an underlying faith in life itself. A faith that life springs from an everlasting supportive energy. I suppose you could argue that this is an optimistic outlook. It is essential to ride successfully through stressful times.

Prosperity is not something you have to slave and scratch for; it is something you can uncover for yourself. The ego will argue that it is hard and out of reach. It isn't at all. Underneath the ego's noise is your confident, trusting inner-self who knows no real harm will ever come to you; life is supporting you 100%. Your financial experience is the reflection of your mind and ego and how they combine to interpret the world as one in which you thrive.

So, if you're focusing on worrying about the economy, politics, or the stock market, remember this, it is not your job to save the world. All you must do is bring forth your exquisite essence. You can accomplish this through appreciation, observing beauty, studying great spiritual masters, meditating, and practicing a sense of presence. When you are aligned with your highest self, your deeds and actions will benefit everyone, not just you. Your contribution will be felt.

Physically, Our Home, Body, and Earth, Abundantly Alive

Our physical environment is our home and our extended body. The earth's respiratory system is the trees, plants and animals exchanging gases. The earth's circulation is the movement of waters through the air and land. And the earth's health is a reflection of our combined health.

On a smaller scale, our home and work environment are a closer reflection of our personal mind/body health. The first chapter on clearing helps with the reduction of clutter; an important part of a healthy environment. A neat home, a feeling of openness, pleasing colors and designs, go a long way to restore our weary selves. The practices of Vastu and Feng Shui not only help you create a home and workplace that promotes health, they can also attract good fortune.

We will assume you've attended to the de-cluttering of your environment and moved on to making it truly healthy. Here are some suggestions:

- Minimize toxins in clothing, furniture, toiletries, food
- Use natural and organic products for cleaning, decorating and utility when possible
- Place live plants in your home
- Live near nature if possible so you can go outside often
- Live near a body of water
- Live where there is clean air

Our physical bodies, of course, need our loving attention and care. It is important to show gratitude for all the body does for us — the feet who carry us where we need to go, our protective skin, our senses, digestion, the incredible dexterity of our hands, our ability to heal from wounds and illnesses, the ability to move, dance and play! We appreciate and honor our bodies by these loving practices. Build a better body!

To find your success it helps to feel energetic, rested, alert, clear headed, with acute senses, aware, and pain free.

I refer back to Ayurveda for time-proven methods to create vitality and wellbeing in the body and mind. Ayurveda is a very deep topic, a vast, ancient, body of knowledge divined long before any other known health system. But it's more than a health system.

So many people around me are suffering, and many would find relief from this health system. It is one of the most fascinating subjects I've ever studied.

The more I study it, the more intrigued I am. It is so beautiful. An elegant way to view our personal systems: physical, intellectual, emotional, and spiritual. It is a consciousness-based philosophy, viewing all that we see and experience in life a result of how we allow consciousness to express through us and how we influence it by our thoughts, actions, and beliefs.

Some basics:

- We are each born with our own individual combination of the elements of life: fire, water, air, space, and earth
- The balance of these at birth is perfect to support each of us in our wellbeing
- As we grow and live our lives, interacting with our environment and others, we can shift away from this ideal balance.
- When this imbalance isn't addressed, over time it can grow into an illness, disease, chronic condition, or emotional illness.

Ayurveda, in a simplistic description, is a system to move the mind and body back to the original balance of elements so the whole being can function the way it was meant to, with one experiencing wellbeing, vitality, joy, and inspiration in their life.

There are three main mind/body types: Vata (air and space), Pitta (fire and water), and Kapha (earth & water).

When a person has a Vata constitution, or air type, they have a tendency to be slim, quick moving, talkative, creative and inspiring. When they get stressed, they may get anxious or worried. If their body develops too much Vata they may get arthritis, degenerative conditions, constipation, all considered to be from too much air/space which are drying. Vata types can tire more easily and should choose gentle exercise like walking and yoga, or they could need joint replacements!

Pitta, or fire types, usually have well developed, athletic bodies, with a sharp intellect, and determined, sometimes intense, personalities. Most leaders are Pittas. Under stress, Pittas may get irritable or angry. Since fire is a dominant element, if a Pitta has too much fire, they may tend to get rashes, heartburn, inflammatory illnesses and heart disease or rheumatoid arthritis. The preferred exercise for a Pitta would be moderate: swimming, biking, yoga etc.

Kapha, or earth types, have a more substantial body, an earthy quality, and they tend to be warm, nurturing, steady and calm. When they learn something, it isn't usually forgotten. Under stress, a Kapha will tend to avoid conflict, often wishing to ignore problems, like sticking their head in the sand, and may get lethargic or depressed. Physically, if too much Kapha type food is in their diet and lifestyle, they will gain weight and have a hard time losing it. They can have sinus issues, diabetes, varicose veins, and edema. Their best form of exercise is more strenuous: weight-lifting, jogging, etc. as they have great endurance. (Once you get them moving!)

Our actions and reactions, our thoughts and feelings, all combine to either support our health or impede it. If you aren't experiencing wellbeing, know that you can find it again.

Western medicine is absolutely critical for urgent care but doesn't address many vague symptoms of imbalance like insomnia, constipation, sadness, lack of motivation or joy in life. Sometimes, the drugs that are prescribed can mask these symptoms without discovering the cause.

Ayurveda can help you discover the cause and address it. It's worked with me quite a few times when I had vague symptoms that a regular doctor would respond with, "You're fine. I can't find anything wrong with you!"

Here is an example, once my skin was itching for weeks and nothing I tried worked. My Ayurvedic physician gave me some herbs and suggestions on diet, and it was gone in three days! He said it was my body trying to detox, so he helped it along. Applying lotions for dry skin, which I thought it was, wouldn't have addressed this at all.

It isn't always quick like this, and in our impatience, we want speedy fixes, but shifting the body and mind back to health can take some time. It may have taken years to become imbalanced, so it makes sense to be patient and focus on a lifetime of healthy practices instead of immediate cures.

Ayurveda is a beautiful science which views humans as an incredible orchestration of energy and information always in flux, morphing into the next thing by perception, from God consciousness into the raw elements, forming the material world and you.

Here are some daily practices that nudge our miraculous bodies toward wellbeing. That means financial success AND a healthy body so we can enjoy a great lifestyle. Given the correct environment, our bodies know just what to do. These are great for all types:

- A daily self-massage called Abhyanga. Easy and not time consuming, it will flush toxins, good for the lymphatic system, and help you relay to your body your appreciation! There is a good video showing how to do this on the website, BanyanBotanicals.com and several other sites.
- Eat only when hungry. Stop eating when 75% full. This enables complete digestion.
- Eat a good breakfast, hearty lunch, and small dinner. Your digestion is strongest at midday. And you will sleep better without overeating at night.
- Don't eat past 7:00 PM
- Bed by 10:30 PM
- Meditate early morning and late afternoon on an empty stomach
- Exercise in the early morning
- Eat a mostly plant-based diet
- Walk on the earth barefoot whenever you can
- Watch sunsets and sunrises—very healing for the eyes

Financially, *Our Financial House*

Before we tackle where our money is and why, let's revisit, according to Ayurveda, how your own mind/body type affects your experience with money.

Here is the description of the three mind/body types along with their responses to money and investing:

VATA: Changeable, creative, lively, artistic, quick moving, expressive with a tendency toward worry and anxiety when they are stressed, (For example, while watching the volatility of the stock market.). An air type may be impulsive and enjoy spending money, often to their own detriment. Once they entertain thoughts of the market going south, or the possibility of flaws in their investment plan, they may get anxious and think they've made a mistake. They may even lay awake worrying about it.

If this sounds like you, do things to create a calmer life. To reassure yourself, create a plan that includes less volatility, stay prudent, and find someone to coach you so when the markets get scary, they help you stick to your plan. The challenge here is to keep yourself from making rash decisions, foiling your long-term goals.

At your worst, you may impulsively jump in and out of the market or withdraw money for an imprudent purchase. But, at your best, you appreciate the philosophy and creativity of a solid, wealth building strategy, along with the security of it. You are extraordinary in the creativity department, so devise the terminology and schematics for your financial plan. Stay away from topics that cause you to worry or obsess about your investments. Go outside and take a walk.

PITTA: Pitta has a high intellect, loves having control, is ambitious, likes luxury and the finer things in life, and often has leadership qualities. When stressed, a Pitta type can get irritable and angry. They are mostly good savers until their competitive nature and desire to look successful causes them to choose big dollar items that are not always best for their overall financial plan.

Once this group understands the portfolio allocations and their options, they rapidly pick one with an objective they like. They are usually good to go until a friend brags about the newest, greatest mutual fund, stock or scheme, which can get under their skin and drive them back into the office to see what is wrong with their portfolio! Patience isn't such a virtue for this group either.

If this sounds like you, use this knowledge to guide you back into financial health. Do everything you can to keep yourself focused on your plan, regardless of what anyone else is doing, or saying! Once you completely understand the reasons for your reactions, keep the vision of your own success in mind. What will work best for you is giving yourself occasional rewards, turning off all volatile economic or financial news that can cause you to become doubtful or irritated (because you can't control the markets) and find things that soothe you. Take up yoga.

KAPHA: These warm, kind-hearted souls are ever-patient, giving, caring, and understanding. They can save like nobody's business. Once they decide on a plan, they are loyal to it. They tend to procrastinate, so the first hurdle is making a decision. Once they do, they are good to go. The downside of being this type, however, is the predisposition to hang onto things too long, and that goes for their money too. They may have too much building up in the bank; it's comfortable, but their money isn't working for them. This is a type of stagnation. If they receive a recommendation to change assets that are in a poor investment, to develop their estate plan, or update beneficiaries, it is easier for a Kapha type to push it down the road. At worst, when things go wrong, they get depressed, which causes even greater withdrawal from needed actions.

If this sounds like you, find ways to get yourself stimulated to take action and tackle these tasks so that you are financially healthy and secure. Find ways to uplift and encourage yourself. You ultimately have more endurance than the other types, so once you do decide on a path, you're well on the way of amassing a rich life. No one can stop you once you build momentum. And it is important for Kapha types to physically move, so get out and run!

No one is solely one of these types. But we all can recognize dominant attributes of one or two in ourselves. Part of a financial advisor's job is to help you devise your goals and strategies and coach you to stick to it when you get in your own way!

How do we prepare and establish our own financial plan? Here are the nuts and bolts of it in the material world:

1) Have it all together: life insurance, health insurance, savings and investment accounts, and an estate and retirement plan.

Be organized! Having your financial life organized makes it manageable. If it is manageable, you are under less stress, right? What a great example of adulthood when you have it together enough to know what documents you need to have in place, if they are all current, and when you need to review them. Do you have a safe deposit box or online storage that holds your important documents? After considering myriad possible scenarios, are you sure you have all of the essential documents in place and up to date?

Here is an example of possible safe deposit contents:

- Life insurance policies
- Home owner's insurance policy
- Mortgage deed or home title and other real estate holdings' documents
- Photos of home contents and valuables for insurance
- A list of your accounts with institutions, account numbers and ownership, including retirement accounts and annuities with beneficiaries listed.
- Will and/or Trust documents
- Durable Family Powers of Attorney in case of incapacity
- Health Care Surrogate Powers of Attorney
- List of personal advisors with contact information: accountant, attorney, and financial planner/advisor.

2) Have Trustworthy Advisors

Do you think the very wealthy handle all their legal, financial, and real-estate dealings on their own? Of course, they don't. They have people who they consider trusted allies with a vested interest in their success.

The professionals work through all future possible events for their clients to make sure they have built an intangible structure that will, to the best of their ability, protect them come what may. There is an accountability factor when working with trusted advisors. We all know that when it is a team effort, we tend to have a greater commitment. When people sit down and come up with their own budget and savings plan, etc. without sharing their intentions or seeking advice—those plans can fade away and be forgotten as soon as something unexpected happens. It is very easy to lose the momentum of a good plan when something knocks you down financially, but if you enlist professionals, you are likely to get back on track more quickly. Something unexpected will always happen because we cannot know what is around the corner.

3. Hire a Coach or Counselor

If you feel you are somehow blocked from financial health yourself, and cannot seem to get a handle on why, coaching may help. Perhaps you have had poor thinking habits, lack of self-confidence, or past conditioning that is holding you back. This is common—who has never felt this way? Clearing your way to better financial health may be fostered by personal or group coaching. I have seen magical transformations in individuals who had a compassionate financial or life coach. There is good reason that the coaching industry is growing. A skilled and qualified coach can assist you in discovering what has been preventing you from the success you desire.

If your concerns are more than just your financial life, if they extend to relationships and personal problems or traumatic history, a good counselor can help.

4. Have Funding for Future Plans

Have a college funding plan for the kids, a retirement plan, and an estate plan. It takes a little time, but once you do it, only a little fine tuning will be needed as your life situations change. Again, take advantage of professionals. Ask your friends for referrals. Interview candidates to get a feel for their approach. You wouldn't want to use a stock trader for long-term wealth creation, or conversely, a conservative money manager for day trading. Referrals usually work well because your friends are people with whom you probably have a lot in common. Find someone you feel will understand you. Many people utilize the services of professionals who use jargon they may not easily comprehend. It is a very thorny job for lawyers, accountants, and advisors to relate difficult material in layman's terms, but that is what they are supposed to do. Make decisions only when you are clear on what they are telling you.

5. Have a Long-Term Vision

This is your map. Know where you want to go. How long do you want to work? How much of your child's college education do you want to pay for? What kind of income do you want to live on during retirement in today's dollars? Do you want to be self-employed by a certain age? Do you have plan B and plan C in place if for some reason you were to lose your job through layoffs or some catastrophe? I know these aren't fun questions and most people put them off, but all you have to do is have something in mind in this regard. As time moves forward your attention and intention will naturally crystallize with the help of your advisors. With life expectancy increasing, we all need to plan for a longer retirement. Do not depend 100% on Social Security. As our growing population swells the retirement ranks, it's uncertain how long the government can continue issuing social security checks.

6. Stay Within a Budget

Spend less than you make. Don't buy things you cannot afford. It is all so simple, common knowledge even, yet everyone at some time has made these mistakes. Once you have mastered the periodic saving of a portion of your income, and watch it grow in value on your statements, it's usually enough incentive to keep it up. There are many automatic ways to painlessly save; namely, 401k or other retirement plan installments deducted from your pay, an automatic investment plan with a mutual fund company that drafts a monthly dollar amount from your bank account, or a brokerage account money market to regularly invest in. Pay yourself first.

7. Reduce Your Debt

Write down all your debt with the interest rates you pay and begin systematically paying them off, with the highest interest rate debt first, then the second highest, and so on. If you have a credit card debt that you are paying 12% on, and a mortgage that you are paying 6% on, pay the credit card off first. That's like giving yourself 12% (you are saving 12%) on your money! You can set up your own debt accelerator by paying some off out of each paycheck instead of waiting for the monthly bill. Go on the internet to find a program to calculate a debt reduction schedule, or have a financial planner help you make the plan.

8. Have Confidence

Once you put your plans in place, or start the process of doing so in earnest, you will clearly see yourself on the path to financial competence and your confidence will grow. You will experience a real peace of mind knowing you are doing your best. No one can guarantee your future or your children's, but you can eliminate many financial casualties that befall thousands, if not millions, of people every year. You will have financial wellbeing, which is high on the Map of Money Consciousness™.

9. Hang With Role Models

Spend time with other successful people! The more you are around these types of people, the more they will absorb those wonderful attitudes. Robert Kiyosaki, in his book *Rich Dad, Poor Dad*, told the story about his best friend's entrepreneurial father. Robert was so greatly influenced by his friend's father that it changed his course in life. Today Mr. Kiyosaki has a multi-million-dollar company and lectures all over the world to show others how they can be financially successful.

And of course, if at all possible, limit your exposure to people with negative beliefs about money.

Affirmation:

My innate wisdom guides me toward the optimum care for my soul, my body, and my assets.

Chapter 6

Commitment & Intention
Holding Ourselves Accountable

"When work, commitment, and pleasure all become one and you reach that deep well where passion lives, nothing is impossible."
– Jean-Jacques Rousseau

"Commitment is what transforms a promise into a reality."
– Abraham Lincoln

This chapter is nothing more than a new start. Tying all the pieces together, wrapping them up with your intentions, and committing to do what is necessary to heal your relationship with money, yourself, and the world. Let's review. How do you see yourself spiritually, physically, and financially now? Are you noticing any connection, coherence, coincidences, dance of the universe, and the results in the material world?

Intention is an energy that begins movement in consciousness, every intention, large or small, strong or weak, affects the whole in a commensurate way. We all have 'good' intentions! But alas, many never come to fruition. Intention is the necessary first step. Then comes commitment. This ensures your intention will turn into action and make changes in the world you live in.

We can bring intentions into our days, into our personal, family, and community lives, and we can make a commitment to follow through on those intentions. We can enlist like-minded friends or a coach to hold us to our plans and intentions. It all begins with intention and ends with Peace of Mind.

What does commitment look like when it comes to:

Spiritually, *Consciousness and Intentions*

Physically, *The Physical Commitments*

Financially, *Financial Commitments, Kick Butt Time*

Spiritually, *Consciousness and Intentions*
Commitment within Consciousness

What does commitment and intention look like under the topic of consciousness? Within this subject we've got the non-physical expanse of energy, personality, emotions, soul, mind, and psychology! Pinning this down to commitment might be like trying to tie something down with a wet noodle. On the other hand, you are not limited! Your goals will shift and change, what you want will change, and after reaching a specific goal you may realize that isn't the end all of accomplishments — there is more!

Let's take inventory. Have any of your ideas about yourself changed?

If I could be anything, I would be _____

If I could do anything, it would be _____

I really admire _____

I am naturally good at _____

My contribution to the world is _____

My friends like me because _____

My heroes are _____

I admire these qualities in people _____

All the qualities you admire are actually those you have within yourself, as well as the qualities in others that bug you! Stretch your ideas about yourself. You're only aware of a small fraction of who you really are. We all have talents waiting in the wings to be brought into our lives.

What are some of the things you can commit to in developing the qualities you admire? Here are a few ideas for you to get you thinking:

- Commit to self-discovery. Witness yourself honestly.
- Spend a little time each day or week to see how you can be more like your heroes and archetypes.
- Write down your intentions and see how you can commit to them.
- Read your commitments before meditation.
- Have one to work on each week.
- Make affirmations and repeat while taking a walk.

Just pick one or two. There are so many ways you can improve, grow, expand and there is no wrong way. But if you attempt to change too much at once you may get discouraged.

Stepping up and taking more responsibility for your situation enables you to climb the levels of money consciousness. Self-direction, self-fulfillment, and self-expansion are all a product of your evolution.

When I left the security of working for a large firm to step out on my own, open my own office, I used one specific technique that was really helpful. I was near terrified to step out on my own, thinking thoughts like, what if my clients won't come with me? What if I use all my savings and it doesn't work? What will my clients or community think? And on and on. So, I used an affirmation I learned from Deepak Chopra, called Self-Referral. Every morning while I jogged down the street, I repeated these phrases:

- I am totally independent of the good or bad opinion of others.
- I am beneath no one, and no one is beneath me.
- I am fearless in the face of any and all challenges.

Here are the complete instructions from Deepak *(used by permission):*

Cultivate Self-Referral

Self-referral is identifying with your inner self – the unchanging essence of your soul. This state has certain characteristics, including an internal sense of joy or wellbeing regardless of what is happening in the exterior world.

In self-referral, you're not attached to outcome or obsessed with power, money, or control; you're in touch with your feelings and you feel what you feel. You're not easily offended and you don't feel superior or inferior.

In self-referral you have infinite freedom and are able to make spontaneous evolutionary choices. You're not anticipating a response and you're not victimized by memory. You're literally in the flow of the evolutionary impulse of the universe.

Exercise: The Fire In Your Eyes

Conscious inner dialogue is a powerful tool for expanding the state of self-referral. Whenever you look in the mirror, even if just for a few seconds, make eye contact with yourself and silently repeat the three principles of self-referral:

- I am totally independent of the good or bad opinion of others.
- I am beneath no one, and no one is beneath me.
- I am fearless in the face of any all challenges.

Look into your eyes to see these attitudes reflected back at you. Look just at your eyes, not at your facial expression. Look for the shine in your eyes that reflects the fire in your soul. If you do this exercise for a few minutes every day, it can create profound shifts in your life.

Physically, *The Physical Commitments*

How can your body, your personal environment, and the material world support you on your path? What impressions are you getting on the 'feedback loop' around you? Do you see space to rise in your world?

What can you commit to now, at this moment, to take better care of your home and your body? We covered the *how* on this in detail in the last chapter.

You can make a list of to-dos to brighten up your living spaces and workspaces. Have the intention to live in beautiful surroundings that speak of who you are but also who you want to be. What improvements can you make? Some ideas:

- Commit to keep your possessions in good working order.
- Commit to get those things that don't work properly out of your environment.
- Commit to reorganize your home workspace.
- Commit yourself to a gentle timeline or completion date for your goals.

And your miraculous wonder of a body? What commitments can you make to 'up' your overall health? What will you do today, this week, this month to ramp up your own care? You could have the intention and commitment to:

- Go to bed at a reasonable time.
- Take a walk outside several times a week.
- Eat more plant-based foods.
- Eliminate snacking in between meals.
- Listen to your body and learn some new self-soothing practices.
- Listen to your favorite music.
- Go to yoga classes or other low impact exercises.

Even better than this, write down what you envision it will be like if you follow what health improvements you know would be good for you. If it is to move more—get off the couch, what will it feel like to take long walks down scenic paths? And when you get home, shower up and put on crisp clean clothes and enjoy your body flushed with improved circulation, pumped lymphatic system, awakened muscles, with an alert mind! That is the immediate reward!

Another category you could put on your list is spending time with friends and associates who may be in the business you'd like to be in.

Financially, *Financial Commitment, Kick in the Butt Time*

So much fear surrounds the idea of money in our world today. If we shift our idea of support from needing money to seeking the experience of wellbeing, money will be there as a secondary form of support. Money follows, it doesn't lead.

We are entering a time where the concept of money is changing. It will still be utilized, but its framing will transform, so that it isn't an end in and of itself. Your experience of a warm loving, healthy, fulfilling life is not set at a dollar amount.

Of course, you have an idea of what makes people financially successful, such as the attitudes, practices, and beliefs they hold that make it more likely. There is also the topic about what drives our economy. Lately it is in vogue, especially in the spiritual community, to slam the entire monetary system because of its flaws. Just know, it is a perfect system that perfectly reflects the mood—optimism/pessimism, hopes and fears—of the masses in the present moment. As we grow, change, and evolve, so will the economic system, naturally.

Can we develop the personal qualities, tendencies, and habits to foster prosperity? Of course.

Unfortunately (or fortunately) it only takes one meeting with new clients to figure out where they are on my map of money consciousness. From body posture when speaking about their financial life, to tone, to repeated sentiments, (stories of helping others with money to no avail, stories of missing out on an inheritance, stories of not finding a job, stories of waiting until too late to save money, and all manner of powerlessness). They may even talk themselves out of having the ability to reach financial health.

I usually focus on explaining what to do to reach financial health and wellbeing. And yet, sometimes it is butt-kicking time. Sometimes people just need a strong look in the mirror to see what they desperately need to change in themselves. So here is the butt-kicking list.

1) Quit making excuses. Stop listing the reasons why you can't.

2) Quit using your family as your excuse. We know you have a tender heart and want to help others, but if you are giving others money you actually need for your financial health, your actions will cause bitterness, resentment, even anger, and you will never be rich enough to be of real help. Be honest with yourself and learn how to tell someone you're not in a position to help them out financially. Find another way to help.

3) Educate yourself

4) Seek higher employment

5) Read

6) Meditate

7) Network

8) Create a vision

What if we treated money like we do our beloved pets?

I've known so many people with lots of money. They aren't especially smart, they don't have some special, secret talent, they just enjoy money. It is sort of like their pet or a hobby. They enjoy watching it grow, enjoy feeding it, they like taking time to pay attention to it, and they get rewarded for this by how much freedom it brings them. They often really like sharing it in various ways.

So, what if we treated money as our special pet? What if we took time to find it a very nice place to nest, encouraging it to grow? What if we fed it regularly? And took out only what it wouldn't miss? And as we aged and matured it did too, along with paying us dividends in the form of income, vacations, and joyful purchases?

Declaration of (Financial) Freedom

What holds us back from the complete freedom we crave? One of the reasons we tell ourselves is that we can't because we don't have enough money, which represents security to most of us.

It pains me to see others suffer in their thinking about money. I know we have all heard how money is just an energy exchange, it isn't a 'thing' at all, just a symbol. But knowing this doesn't seem to help.

For all the good that money can do, we still see misguided uses of it. If we have a good amount, we worry about the safety of it and our ability to hang on to it. If we don't have enough, it looms over us like an impending storm, the lack of it ready to create a crisis. It takes over our thoughts and we worry about the future. Certainly, money must be there!

Someday, in the not too far future, I think we will have organically transitioned to a different system of exchange. One that honors each person, and every effort brings in response some type of acquisition. Each acquisition or service used creates a deficit that is balanced by a person's inherent gifts and talents. The media and internet teem with projections of a terrible collapse, but fear not, this will more likely be a slow and gradual evolution, not some cataclysmic financial tsunami.

What do we do until then? The quickest, easiest way to prosper as an individual is to grow in your awareness of the infinite support the universe is availing you, right now.

The horrors in the world are of our own making. Know that we are part of society and responsible for that which we rail against. Taking responsibility is the first step. There was a group of activists on kayaks filling a bay to protest against oil companies, yet they were on plastic boats made from petroleum. They were denying their own complicity by utilizing a product from an industry they were objecting to.

1) Take responsibility for your energetic contribution to the less-than-ideal circumstances of the world. It is your unexamined beliefs and assumptions that perpetuate the status quo. When you dwell in worry and doubt, when you embrace an 'against' position, when you hate the 'haters', hate the corporations, or

hate the government, it adds to the conflicted state of the world. Discover the peace that exists deep within your being so that it may be extended out into the world as a healing balm.

2) Become aware of your criticism of others who happen to be wealthy. It isn't a character flaw to be prosperous, it is merely a result of their beliefs about what is possible. Among the wealthy is a wide range of maturity levels and spiritual awareness. Wealth is independent of what you may think is a 'good' person. The character of a person is exhibited by how they live, how they contribute and show kindness, not whether they are wealthy or not. You will hold financial success at bay if you regard wealthy people as corrupt, evil, selfish, etc.

3) Help lift others up. One of the shortcuts to security is helping others become secure and prosperous. And realize security is found within, not without. If you can show others how they can trust in themselves, trust in life, trust their inspiration and passions, you will be lifted too. If you find this type of security, money will follow and flow naturally and it will be a nonevent.

4) Focus on using your life as your unique expression, being you as completely and fearlessly as you possibly can. This will take you places you're not even aware of right now. Delve into the discovery of all that you are. The resources, ideas, people, energy, events, and doorways will all show up at the perfect time. When you are moving in alignment with your highest path it will become so strong, the creative impulse so intense, you will have no other option but to engage in it fully.

5) Ask for guidance. Your inner being and your guides, angels and loved ones on the Other Side are awaiting your requests. They are circling you, waiting for you to notice their messages. They are subtle and could be easily discounted or doubted. If it occurs to you, it is a message, a sign it is or can be. They come in whispers in your mind, your eyes landing on a certain phrase, a stranger with news, a sudden urge to create something, all directing you toward your destination.

6) There is so much in this life to explore, learn and discover and the greatest discovery of all is finding your own divine nature! Then, when you have awakened to your true self, money is nothing you need to worry about.

You've been given so much information. Take your time, and when you feel clear, fill your My Goals and Financial Plan Worksheet to build your own financial plan.

My Goals & Financial Plan Worksheet

Essence is the result attaining the goal, the overall emotional comfort it will bring.

Example:

Spiritually financial health means <u>To have my passion and purpose support me financially.</u>

Essence of having that is <u>I will feel fulfilled finding my right place in the world.</u>

1. Spiritually financial health
   means _____
   Essence of having that
   is _____

2. Physical financial health
   means _____
   Essence of having that
   is _____

3. In money terms, financial health
   means _____
   Essence of having that
   is _____

Assets & Liabilities Balance Sheet

ASSETS

- List your bank accounts and balances
- Retirement accounts and balances
- Life insurance and annuity cash values
- Real-estate properties and values
- Precious metals, cryptocurrency, NFTs etc. values
- Other

LIABILITIES

- Outstanding personal loans
- Credit card debt
- Mortgages
- Auto loans

Accumulation

How much do I want to have in a financial emergency/safety fund? *(3 to 6 months income needs)* _____

What is my discretionary money left over from my income after bills are met? _____

How much am I saving for retirement per month? _____

What is my goal for: *(Can be savings growth, big purchase, a house, vacation money, children's education funds, etc.)*

1 Year from today? _____

5 Years from today? _____

10 Years from today? _____

What income in today's dollars do I want to have in retirement? Figure on taking about 4 or 5 % of the retirement funds balance, plus social security, plus an annuity income or pension payouts. To see how much you will need from your retirement funds to produce your income:

Example:

Social Security amount: (go to www.ssa.gov/myaccount/ to find your estimate)

Desire $7,000 per month

Social security payment	*$2,200*
Pension	*$1,200*
Total	*$3,400*
Need	*$7,000*
Short fall	*$3,600*

Each $100,000 invested in a balanced mutual fund account
withdrawing 4% will give you
$4,000 a year or $333.00 per month
It will take $1,100,000 to make up the $3,600 per month
$1,100,000. X 4% = 43,200 per year, divided by 12 equals
$3,600+ per month

It is an excellent idea to meet with a financial advisor to set
this up. Don't try to do it yourself when the time comes. So
now you know you need one million one hundred thousand in
your retirement savings in this example. There are multiple
calculators for retirement savings, and you can plug in what
you are saving per year, guesstimate the earnings, and pick a
retirement age. It will tell you what you need to save.

What I intend to save monthly now:

For building up my safety net/emergency fund $ _____

For my children's education fund $ _____

For a future large purchase $_____

For retirement $ _____

For retirement you can have your employer withhold an amount
from your paycheck to go directly to a retirement fund, as well as
a savings account with many employers!

You can also set up a mutual fund and have the mutual fund
company draft funds from your checking monthly to be invested
in the fund. Of course, we recommend using an advisor to guide
you if needed. That is probably a good idea.

You have all the information now to develop a financial plan for yourself and hopefully it is much more than that. It will be a platform to tell the story of you.

Write it out as a story in your own words.

Example:

I, _____ began this journey knowing nothing, and I came to this point knowing what I want to do with my life; how I will commit to the plans I've made, how I am to be in this world, how I pledge to care for myself and my loved ones in the highest way possible.

I will always be on the lookout to fulfill my purpose in new and exciting ways.

I intend to save _____ % of my income.

I intend to create a retirement fund and invest _____ monthly.

I will save _____ for my children's education.

I will hire experts where my expertise is lacking.

Chapter 7

The Map of Money Consciousness™

Here we are in the last bit. I hope you've realized it isn't so much about money at all. It is really a path of self-discovery.

Spiritual principles explain how that which we resist and judge harshly is actually our own projections of our suppressed traits, the ones we don't want to believe we have. We see those with power and money often as oppressors, evil-doers, or just plain selfish, which, in turn, puts us in the role of victim. It is a game. There isn't validity in this victim role. Their being rich does not reduce our possibilities.

In the broad spectrum of levels of human consciousness, the acquisition of money is spread across them all. The *Map of Money Consciousness*™ illustrates a different consciousness, one associated with our relationship to money.

On a deep level, we know that rich people aren't 'bad' just by being successful, and corporations aren't 'evil', yet that attitude has gained great popularity—again. I've seen this a few times in my career. When people are suffering, they look outside of themselves to see who to blame. The ones in the spotlight are easy: the corporations who have executives making poor decisions for our culture and health, the arrogant elites who seem oblivious to the needs of employees and others.

Some people who climb to great success may begin their path with a high level of consciousness, but the rush of power causes them to fall away from their own inner awareness; the consciousness that opens compassion, empathy, and self-reflection. But that is a minority, albeit a noticeable, 'in the news' minority. Reality shows, 24-hour cable news, and titillating internet stories all combine to create a story about 'rich' people. Most are people just doing the best they can, like everyone else.

We value stuff so much in our western society. We envy others who acquire lots of stuff. I've seen people who are addicted to attaining stuff. No matter how many houses, cars, or boats they buy, they continue to look for the next thing that will give them a charge, making them feel good about themselves. It isn't about money at all.

On the flip side are those who use their lack of money as an excuse to not try, to stay where they are, not wanting to move into that uncomfortable zone that would cause them to change, preferring to blame someone else.

YET—

It doesn't matter how much money you have. What matters is, how much peace you have. How much wellbeing are you experiencing? How are your relationships? Do you appreciate what is before you, right now? This is abundance. No one is taking this away from you unless you let them.

Take the Money Map quiz again (in the beginning of the book) and see the Key action to move from where you are to the next level! See if you've moved up just reading this book!

The Map of Money Consciousness™ with KEYS

Recall the *Map* is a scale that is designed to explain the graduating levels of understanding about how money works, showing the experience of individuals at each consciousness level.

What determines a position on the scale is a combination of habitual thinking, beliefs, raw intelligence, and emotional intelligence. When these are combined you can see a developing financial maturity. For true fulfillment that includes financial 'harmony' (beliefs, desires, and purpose all blend) one needs to have a well-defined understanding of human behavior, intra- and inter-relationship competence, economic knowledge, confidence in self, and inspired action.

Key: How to move to the next level.

Level One
Blame/Despair/Apathy

Some find themselves in poverty, unemployed or meagerly employed, and embrace the view of victimhood on the world stage of life. They may feel helpless to change circumstances. They blame their situation on others; family, employer, community, 'them', or government leaders. They are resigned to this reality and don't have any hope it will change. It is extraordinarily difficult to raise oneself out of this level, though with a life changing event, they may transcend it. Here, if one happened to win the Lottery it would most likely be gone within two years. Often these kinds of personalities have no money skills and lack the emotional skills as well. They feel the world is conspiring against them. Wealthy people are viewed in mythic proportions; it isn't 'real life' to them.

Key: ACTION

Become aware of your ability to change your circumstances, wake up, get motivated, and take action to get things done. Also, learn to do physical activities that change your environment, and a big one, become employed. Finding role models will very much help do this. Take some action, no matter how small, every day.

Level Two

Fear/Anxiety

Those on this level may be more aware of their situation and have an idea that they 'should' be able to do better, yet still fear the unknown, fear taking chances and have anxiety over change. This is a big hurdle for people in this category. This can all be unconscious; they feel anxiousness surrounding money but can't quite define what is holding them back, or there is depression blocking forward movement. It also corresponds with a lack of trust that life will sustain them. Some can be limited by habitual thinking and only see a way out in magical terms. They may not have faith in their own ability to create a comfortable life. Perhaps they learned this from parents or other significant adults as they were growing up. They resist feeling hopeful in order to avoid disappointment. When money happens to come their way, it seems to slip right through their fingers. They are in financial in chaos.

Key: OVERCOMING FEAR

Fear + action = self-esteem. The key here is to be aware of the fear. Get in touch with this fear/anxiety, accept it and appreciate the safety it has provided in the past, then begin to move beyond it. Define a goal, an attainable but perhaps frightening one, and practice moving through those scary steps. Find a coach or counselor. Realize that the fear is self-created. Ask "What would happen if?" Baby steps.

Level Three

Desire/Craving

At this level people are moving beyond apathy and debilitating fear, so desires naturally spring up. Instead of deadening desires or withdrawing from them, they welcome aspirations into their awareness. They like to entertain bigger ideas and begin to dream of a grander way of life. Money naturally becomes more of a focus in their plans. Checking and savings accounts are becoming mastered, as well as steady employment. They find themselves in a situation of denial for the bulk of their desires, because they may still lack the basic knowledge about money that can enable them to accomplish more. Their resentment of others who have more success is still present and interestingly, that holds them back as well. Envy is often a manifestation of an inner sense of one's own unworthiness.

Key: I AM WORTHY

Go to classes offered by banks, credit unions, brokerage firms and/or advisors, financial planners. Begin your education. Become familiar with financial terms. The whole world is opening up for you. Know that you can be, do and have what your heart desires.

Level Four

Anger/Aggression

At this level there is a dramatic change for some people as they become more aware of the part they play in their own lives. At this level anger shows up and gives them the energy to change their situation. The apathy is gone. It takes an enormous amount of effort to rise up out of a Level Three lifestyle to a higher one. The anger is usually projected out onto others but most likely stems from anger turned inward. A realization begins to percolate that action must be taken and they need to become more aggressive to overcome all the obstacles before them. They need to learn the rules of money. At this level, the anger provides the impetus which makes it possible to continue up the scale.

Key: ENERGY

Learn to use the energy in a positive way. Focus that newfound energy toward goals and desires. You are creating momentum here. Sliding back is becoming unlikely.

Level Five

Courage/Optimism

There is relief here. There is great hope and a feeling of inspiration. Budgeting is mastered. Better employment, a retirement plan, and a healthy curiosity about how money works has become part of the fabric of their lives. They've crossed a defining line where financial disasters are less frequent. People who've reached this level have developed a sense of curiosity about money that can act as protection against commonly made financial mistakes. Not only have they learned about banking and retirement planning but they're also looking at other ways to make their money grow. Their ears are open and they're thinking about ways to manifest more financial security. Though they still have trepidations, they feel empowered. Financial Health is emerging.

Key: APPRECIATION

Look how far you've come! To go to the next level, it is important to pat yourself on the back and honor your path so far. Focus on all the good in your life. Bring appreciation into everything you do.

Level Six

Satisfaction/Trust

At this level people are understandably satisfied. They are learning how to build financial security, maximize their earnings through saving and investing and building good credit. They are careful with purchases and investments. They have mastered delaying gratification which is a necessary component on the way to financial independence. They are beginning to experience the freedom a sustainable faith in their future brings. They know their future is in their own hands and feel up to the challenge. They trust themselves and trust their growing knowledge, but are still a bit hard on themselves, thinking they should do more, know more, and so on.

Key: PURPOSE

To move to the next level, delve into why you are here. What are your strengths? How might you be better served? Develop long-term and short-term plans. Accept yourself and all your attributes, whether seen as good or not so good. Work on self-love and self-knowledge which will take you the rest of the way!

Level Seven

Acceptance/Forgiveness/Giving

Now we are beginning to move onto the downside of the bell curve. The people that have risen to this level are discovering how the economy really works. They've begun to develop a more complete understanding of the free market system, mortgages, credit card companies, and taxes; and are secure in their chosen career. They can look back at their own past choices and understand that they did the best they could with the information they had at that time. So, they can accept their current situation, assess where they want to go, and implement a long-term financial plan. They know their talents, strengths, and have a sense of purpose. They have a forgiving attitude toward themselves and others. They are able to recognize what makes people financially successful and can plainly see why some fail. Blaming others for their situation is unlikely at this stage. A new generosity also begins to emerge that goes beyond focusing on the family and extends outwardly toward community and charity. Financial harmony is possible for this and the upper levels.

Key: STEP OUT

Find your unique passion and go forth and bring it to the world. Know there is no such thing as failure, only challenges. You are ready now.

Level Eight
Wisdom/Abstraction/Reason

Wisdom is knowledge that is internalized and becomes a part of you. It becomes innate. When this is developed with a focus on the subject of economics, a person can successfully run scenarios of financial undertakings through their heads, playing the "What will happen if..." game. Creative expression with finance and business become common here. Failures certainly can occur because they gave it a shot, but here again, a person at this level knows there will be no gain without risk. Until this stage, ventures into business ownership are often unsuccessful. The wisdom necessary to sense various outcomes isn't completely matured until level eight. There is an expansive understanding of human nature which is essential in successful commerce. A strong desire to serve, and a passion for a chosen field becomes more significantly present.

Key: MEANING

Discover what money means to you. Gain more knowledge by finding ways to make money work for you instead of the other way around. Realize money is just spending energy which we barter for all day long. Envision a bountiful income and search your psyche to find why you may be withholding that from yourself. As you do, the reasons fall away, your fear starts to vanish.

Level Nine

Self-Actualization

Now an understanding of the deeper meanings surrounding money start to become clearer as do the integral role emotions play in one's experience with it. A person at this level has mastered the emotional side of money. They assume a feeling of security and no longer worry about material things. They can invest with confidence, review and adjust financial plans, create an estate plan, and participate in some type of service. They've often learned the skill of creating a flow of income that is not dependent on their actions; the money comes in whether they show up to work or not. This is called passive income. Business owners, real estate investors, and security investors can fit in here if they have achieved true meaning and purpose in their lives.

Key: ALLOW

You're just about there! You can hang out here for as long as you are having fun! To go to the next level happens naturally while you're having a great time!

Level Ten

Illumination

Money becomes a natural means to support one's *purpose*. As this person goes out into the world money isn't a focus at all. People flock to support this type of person because of what they represent; hope, knowledge, and inspiration. Great religious leaders, great teachers and other types of leaders are carried on a wave of contributions. Some who attain this level are overcome with greed and fall back several levels. Some on this level retreat happily to live with or without large amounts of money. They have truly 'transcended' their material desires.

Of course, most of you who are reading this will fall somewhere in the middle. Just getting to 6 or 7 is a *real accomplishment*. Having a map can show you where you might want to go. If you want to go to the next level, hang out with others that are on that one.

My Last Message to You

You can gain wealth by working hard, taking risks, continually moving up the ladder, grasping and maneuvering, trying to change yourself for the world. You can suck up the demeaning boss's abuse, bear the slights and lack of recognition along the way. By shear force and dogged determination, you just might become one of the 'successful' ones. I saw this in the brokerage industry, the unfailing loyalty to the company, the acceptance of grueling projects, ungodly long, suffering hours, even sometimes throwing co-workers under the bus. And when you get the corner office, you've made it. Or have you? How much grace is in your life? Peace? Light-heartedness?

On the other hand, what if you followed joy? What if you conducted your life in a way that reflected love? What if you held your wellbeing as a priority, making decisions by taking into account whether they will move you toward more wellbeing, or further away?

A person moving toward their wellbeing, with a holistic approach to self-care, and a practice connecting themselves to the underlying flow of their own divine guidance, will gain prosperity, in whatever form that means to them. It is all created in the moment-by-moment choices we are presented with throughout our day. With a clear head and engaging vitality, we are ready to take on new challenges. Our inner guidance assists our decisions. Our self-knowledge moves us through the fear of going in a new direction. Our maturity helps us know when and who to ask for help.

When I finally, finally faced the fact that the corporate world was making it difficult for me to reach my own wellbeing (as I stated in Chapter 4), I started exploring other options. I researched, read books, and attended spiritually based programs. I spoke with other advisors who left the corporate world to become independent, running their own business. Then I did too, and never looked back. That was over 20 years ago. What is funny is that when you are running your own venture, whether you work 30 or 70 hours a week, it just flies by, because you are filled with a passion for the work you are doing. The energy it takes is abundantly available.

You don't need to start a business yourself to reach prosperity and wellbeing. It may mean doing your own thing in your off hours. It could be writing, acting, volunteering, teaching others, picking up a part time job in a field you are attracted to. The options are endless. And any one of them could lead you to your prosperity. It all begins with caring for yourself.

Keep your vision to yourself, or share only with those who would be supportive. Find that which gives you passion. Never give up!

The Map of Money Consciousness™

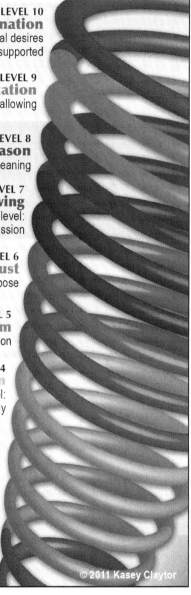

LEVEL 10
Illumination
disappearance of material desires
purpose is effortlessly supported

LEVEL 9
Self-Actualization
key to transcending this level: allowing

LEVEL 8
Wisdom • Abstraction • Reason
key to transcending this level: meaning

LEVEL 7
Acceptance • Forgiveness • Giving
key to transcending this level:
stepping out with passion

LEVEL 6
Satisfaction • Trust
key to transcending this level: purpose

LEVEL 5
Courage • Optimism
key to transcending this level: appreciation

LEVEL 4
Anger • Aggression
key to transcending this level:
use energy positively

LEVEL 3
Desire • Craving
key to transcending this level: I am worthy

LEVEL 2
Fear • Anxiety
key to transcending this level:
overcome fear

LEVEL 1
Blame • Despair • Apathy
key to transcending this level: take action

© 2011 Kasey Claytor

Acknowledgements

This book took many years to write. My family listened to me kindly as I sporadically worked on it in between my business commitments and writing other books. It wasn't easy, and I have great gratitude to them for their assistance. Especially Bill, my husband, who allowed me to work away in my home office as he took charge of everything so I wouldn't be disturbed. And to my son, Aaron, whose support and encouragement means so much.

And to my friends, Julie Schueler and Dawn Lopez, who asked me how the book was going, and gave me their help, continuing support and encouragement. A special thank you for my friend and mentor, Donna Miesbach, who was always there to assist and give guidance.

To all those who have taught me, helped me and guided me; Karen Wolny, Mark Anthony, Hema Vyas, Dr. Deepak Chopra, Dr. David Simon, Elyse Hope Killoran, Dr. Vijay Jain, Roxann Morin, and Alistair.

A huge thank you to all the money management clients I have had over the last many years. Especially those who've become coaching clients, showing courage and willingness to do the hard work to raise their money consciousness. I have learned an enormous amount from all of you.

Finally, to all my teachers and authors, whose work has pulled me forward and given me the tools and practices that have enriched my life so that I can share them all with you. Mike Dooley, Parmahansa Yogananda, Dr. Norman Vicent Peale, Michael Singer, Anita Moorjani, Brent BecVar, Eckart Tolle, Louise Hay and all those mentioned in the bibliography.

About Kasey J. Claytor

Kasey is the founder of Osprey Money Management LLC, an advisory firm that breaks the stereotypes of financial guidance, taking an all-encompassing approach to add a new dimension to a successful investment program for her clientele.

With over thirty-five years of experience and success, Kasey has mindfully developed a comprehensive approach to financial advising in all areas of investment, retirement, college funding, estate wealth transfer, wealth building and wealth coaching.

The financial industry's notoriously stressful environment has led Kasey to research ways to find peace of mind.

Claytor believes that the power to grow in self-knowledge and awareness makes desired situations possible, and her mission is to guide others toward transformation into their true selves. A lifelong meditator, Claytor earned her certification as a meditation instructor through the Chopra Center for Wellbeing in Carlsbad, CA. She is also an Ayurvedic Consultant, and has studied methods to enrich, enliven, and bring wellbeing to her readers, meditation students, and clients.

As a result, she writes and offers workshops on ways to add healthy balance to our lives, reduce stress, and find wellbeing.

Other books by Kasey Claytor:

Fiction

The God of Anna, (Under the name of Kasey Greenhoe)
The Light of Grace

Children's Books

Pinky and the Magical Secret He Kept Inside

Poetry

I know...Me Too

Non-Fiction

The 7 Laws of Raising Financially Independent Kids
Spiritual Will & Legacy

A Brief Bibliography

"A Christmas Story" 81
"A course in Miracles" The quote is from *A Course in Miracles*, copyright ©1992, 1999, 2007 by the Foundation for Inner Peace, copyright holder and publisher, 448 Ignacio Blvd., #306, Novato, CA 94949, acim.org" 78
Antoine de Saint Exupery 37
Banyan Botanicals 158, 151
Beck, Dr. Don 147
Bhagavad Gita 96, 147
Bible, The 94, 104
Brantley, Dr. Jeffery 120
  "Mindfulness-Based Stress Reduction Program"
Buddhism 14
Cameron, Julia 81
  "The Right to Write"
Chadron, Pema 113
Chopra, Dr. Deepak 94
Christianity 14
Descartes, Rene 17
Duke Center for Integrative Medicine 120
Dyer, Dr. Wayne 45
EFTs 56
Emerson, Ralph Waldo 91
Fama, Eugene 139
French, Kenneth 139
Gilman, Charlotte Perkins 113
Graves, Clare 22
  "Spiral Dynamics"
Hawkins, Dr. David 22, 64, 74, 77, 100, 147
  "I, Reality & Subjectivity" 77
  "Levels of Human Consciousness" 22
  "Map of the Scale of Consciousness" 195
  "Power vs. Force" 64
  "The Eye of the I" 74
Ibbotson, Roger 139
Kasey Claytor's web site 23, 78
Katie, Byron 100, 127
  "The Work"
Kingston, Karen 48
  "Clear Your Clutter with Feng Shui"
Kiyosaki, Robert 166
  "Rich Dad, Poor Dad"

Kornfield, Jack 100
  "After the Ecstasy, the Laundry"
Lao-tzu 59, 104, 105, 107
Lashley, Karl 40
"Leave It to Beaver" 11
Lincoln, Abraham 167
Markowitz, Harry 139
Miphom, Sakyon 44
  "Turning the Mind Into an Alley"
Morningstar 109
Nestor, James 103
  "Breath"
Peale, Dr. Norman Vincent 114, 121
  "The Power of Positive Thinking"
Penfield, Wilder 41
Pickford, Mary 98
Ponder, Catherine 79
  "Dark Night of the Soul" 78
  "Universal Forgiveness Treatment" 79
Quinn, Jane Bryant, Columnist 135
Rig Veda 147
Rousseau, Jean-Jacques 167
Schmidt, Helmut 81
Science of Mind 13
September 11th 110, 136
Seth books 13
Singer, Michael 100
Smith, Adam 106
  "The Wealth of a Nation"
St. Francis of Assisi 96
Tao te Ching 59, 104
Tolle, Eckhart 100
Unity Church Worldwide 79
Wall Street 108
Walsh, Dr. David 134
  National Institute on Media and the Family
Washington Post 135
Wing, R.L. 59, 104, 105
  "The Tao of Power"
Wilbur, Ken 22, 147, 148
  "Integral Psychology"

Index

Made in the USA
Columbia, SC
27 September 2023